My Kidhood

JOHN A. MARSZALEK

DEDICATION

To everyone who helped me through
my kidhood, and made it easier
for me to move on.

Table of Contents

Introduction

The following adventures and stories are about me, John Marszalek, a little innocent kid from Chicago who, with a lot of luck, somehow survived kidhood and made a mild success of himself in his adult life. The story does not go too far beyond childhood because, quite frankly, adulthood has not turned out to be as interesting.

Most adults and that includes me, who are beyond middle age share a common regret: "Why didn't I ask my parents about their early lives when I had the chance? There's so much I don't know."

Yes, it would have been so simple to do it back then, and our parents surely would have welcomed both our undivided attention and the opportunity to reminisce. But what usually happens is; we wait too long to ask these questions and our parents are either no longer available or, sadly, can't remember.

So to save my kids and grandkids from having similar regrets, I decided to document my young life so if someday they should be interested, much of the information would still be readily available even though I would not.

These stories cover my life during the twenty-or-so years that are centered on the 1950s. I do not go beyond my early-adult years because, shortly thereafter I got married and my wife knows everything that happened to me since. (If you don't believe me, just ask her.)

By the way, one sure way to know you are dying is if the following happens: you are sick in bed — possibly in a hospital — and your kid comes by and says "hey mom/dad, tell me about the time you were ten years old."

It's definitely over.

1

Beginning

I was born in Chicago in mid-December on a very important day in American history. The date was December 12, 1936 — Frank Sinatra's 21st birthday. So while Frankie and his band buddies were getting legally drunk for the first time, my parents were in a taxi on their way to Saint Ann's Hospital.[1] As a point of reference, my mother was 36 years old and my father was 49.

It also must have been a very important day for my parents because, as I mentioned, they took a taxi to the hospital. The reason I bring up this fact is it was one of the few times that they traveled any distance within the city without taking a streetcar.

The family did not own a car, and riding in one was a treat that was always associated with a major event

---

1 Oddly enough, this was the same hospital where my wife-to-be was born three years later, maybe even in the same room.

such as a funeral or a wedding. In this case, the major life-changing event was the impending birth of their second son.

After spending a few days in the hospital which was the norm at the time, I was brought home to the second-floor apartment in a small rented house at 2020 West Erie Street on the near-West Side of the city, not too far from Chicago's downtown area.

All houses in the neighborhood were small. They were one- and two-story wooden structures jammed very closely to one another, almost like little detached townhouses.

Each house was separated from its neighbor by a narrow passageway that ran from the street, through a tiny backyard and finally to an alley that extended the full length of the block. (Chicago residents refer to this passageway between houses as a "gangway.") When I moved in, the houses on the block were already ancient. The few that are still standing today are well over 100 years old.

Recently, however, many parts of Chicago have been rediscovered and rehabilitated by rich, young folks looking to live closer to their offices downtown. This is what has happened to most of the houses along Erie Street. Many of the old wooden structures were torn down and replaced by sturdier brick units in either the single- or multiple-family style.

At the time I moved into the Erie Street house it had been my parents' home for several years. After they got married they lived with my father's sister's family for several months. It's no surprise that this arrangement got very uncomfortable quickly and they struck out on their own to Erie Street, not too far from my aunt's home. It also was the house in which my brother Edward spent his entire short life. I never met him because, like me, my brother was an only child.[2]

My brother Edward's life story is short and quite sad. When he was an infant, he fell out of his carriage and probably suffered brain damage which did not show up for a while. As a result of the fall, he developed epilepsy in his early childhood.

My mother told me of his dreadful seizures. Because he also was considered to be "slow," it is easy to imagine that he had a difficult time in school with both his studies and with fellow classmates.

For some reason, my mother saved all his report cards. I discovered them packed away in the basement when I was still in grade school. I remember that his grades were not very good, actually worse than mine, which is hard to believe.

Despite this documented hard evidence to the contrary, my mother insisted he had been a brilliant student and an exemplary, well-behaved son. She always compared this fictional Edward to me, and I, of course, always came out wanting. This "departed angel" was always presented as someone who should serve as my idol.

---

2 "My brother was an only child" was Tom Smothers' favorite line which he used often on The Smothers Brothers Show, a popular TV program of the 70s. When I first heard it, I said "hey, me too!"

As a young child, I consistently failed to match up to the Edward my parents remembered. I must have sensed there was really no way for me to compete, so after a short while, I didn't even try.

Then, as if by magic, the comparisons ceased altogether when I passed my tenth birthday, Edward's age when he died. Very little mention was made of Edward after that. There was no other son, alive or dead, with whom I could be compared. I was now out there alone, moving along a portion of life's path that "Saint Edward" had not trod.

I have no active memories of our first house. Our small family lived there for about four years when an event of mixed blessings occurred. My father (whom I called Tata) had an accident while working as a factory hand at a bedspring manufacturing company.

How he broke his leg, I don't know, but the mishap resulted in some time off with pay plus a lump-sum insurance settlement. This windfall payment of about $1,000 enabled my parents to put a substantial down payment on a house about 20 blocks to the west on a street named Kamerling Avenue and got us out of the semi-slum conditions of Erie Street. Although our next house was not fancy, nor in the suburbs, it was in a newer, more modern neighborhood. We were moving up!

The family lived on Kamerling for only a few years before moving to an even newer neighborhood located a few blocks away on Crystal Street. The primary reason for this move was to cut the distance I had to walk to school in half. (More on this later.)

One thing I failed to mention about the Erie Street environment was that it was a bonafide Polish ghetto. Almost all the neighbors were

Polish as were the neighborhood's storekeepers. Some of the adults knew each other from the "old country" and some even came from the same Polish villages and towns. Once they got to the United States they joined various Polish social clubs, each of which was regional in nature. There was an active competition between them. Each club considered itself better than any other due to the obvious superiority of the represented Polish countryside.

The members of the more sophisticated clubs were typically from the larger cities within Poland such as Krakow and Warsaw. Other organizations had rosters consisting mostly of former peasant farmers. My parents belonged to a club that represented the Southern region of Poland where the "Gorale" or "Hill People" lived. I learned early in life that I was related to Polish hillbillies.

These clubs had many social activities and provided the immigrants with some semblance of unity with the Mother Country. Belonging to one or more of these clubs somehow blunted the deep guilt they all felt for abandoning their birthplaces and families, even though leaving Poland was truly the sensible thing to have done. I am forever grateful to them that they did.

On Erie Street, Polish was the language of the street, home, radio, newspaper, school, and church. It also was my first and only language. We spoke only Polish at home and when I met other little kids, we played games and yelled at each other and called each other names, all in Polish. This is where I acquired the nickname of Jasiu (Ya-shoe), which is the Polish diminutive of John. I was called Jasiu by both adults and kids until starting high school.

The new neighborhood was a little different, and so were its inhabitants. Although Polish was spoken here and there, it was not the native language. I had to learn how to speak English in order to communicate with my new playmates, and I learned it through trial and error on the street. Not surprisingly, within a very short time, I was better at it than either of my parents, neither of whom ever really caught on to this complicated, foreign tongue.

The language they spoke to each other, however, was not pure Polish as I later found out. So much of what these immigrants encountered in their new daily life was very different from what they had known back in Poland. Because they knew of no Polish equivalents, they simply Polish-ized the English words by changing the endings to conform to the rules of Polish grammar and used them in conversation. This was done to such an extent that even some English words that had obvious Polish equivalents were adopted into the vernacular.

A prime example is the word boy. The Polish language has a perfectly good word for boy (chlopiec), but it was discarded in favor of the shortened, pseudo-Polish version (boi or boisik) which was then used almost exclusively.

In addition to adapting English words, there were several German words in everyday conversation. The most common was the use of the German "ja" for "yes," instead of the Polish "tak." (I attribute this to the fact that during WWI a detachment of German soldiers set up camp right across the road from my mother's house. Their proximity must have had some influence on her, both good and bad as described in a later chapter.)

The houses along Kamerling Avenue were large, identical, two-story brick units arranged in perfectly straight lines along both sides of the street. Each house had two separate apartments (known as flats), one upstairs and the other downstairs. Each house also had a full basement and a nice-sized yard. They all, of course, were separated by gangways, each about six-feet wide.

The two-flat feature meant the owner could live in one apartment and rent the other, a very good income source. Often, many of the "really Polish" landlords lived in the less-desirable second-floor flat and rented out the lower, more expensive unit. My parents did not do that. Anyway, not at first.

By buying the house my parents instantly switched roles from lowly tenant to all-powerful landlord. Being the landlady or "baska" (pseudo-Polish for boss-lady) made my mother very happy. She was well suited for the part and just loved the concept of collecting rents and meddling in the lives of her tenants. She played the role with great gusto for nearly the rest of her life.

How much that first house cost, I don't know. The purchase did, however, require the acquisition of the dreaded mortgage, the idea of which my parents hated. Having to owe all that money to a bank made them nervous because, after all, the memories of the Depression were still very fresh. They felt this heavy burden had to be lifted quickly, so the loan had to be paid off well in advance of its due date. Then, as now, the only solution was the wife had to go to work.

My mother had no marketable skills. She did, however, know someone who had a night job cleaning business offices downtown.

Times were still tough after the Depression and throughout the 1930s, so it took some pull to get any job, even as a lady-janitor.

She learned from a Polish club member that a job was available at the Marshall Field Department Store cleaning the corporate offices. As in many other times in her life, she took the direct approach: she wrote a letter to the President of the company asking for the job.

I don't know what was in the letter, but I do know it had to have been written in cursive and in Polish. When she went in for the interview, she learned that the letter had been laboriously translated into English by someone within the organization and the interview itself was conducted through a translator.

The hiring manager was either impressed by her spunk or was moved by her desperation and gave her the job. She soon began working nights (5 pm to 2 am) downtown while my father worked the day shift in a factory.

I was left with the upstairs tenant lady for the a few hours after my mother went to work and before my father came home. In reality, though, the tenant didn't watch me very carefully and I was left to my own devices to wander around the neighborhood most of the time.

I remember once hiding in our back yard in a "fort" I had built out of a large cardboard box. Just before my father came home, the tenant lady called for me to make sure I was there when he arrived. I did not answer her repeated calls and stayed hidden in the box while peeking through a hole I had made.

I was very amused as I watched her running around, frantically searching for her missing charge. She really was afraid that I was lost and was about to tell my father the bad news when I jumped out of the box to greet them both. I suspect I got spanked for this cleverness.

The pre-war years were a tough time for both my parents as well as for other families in our economic situation. I don't believe we had a refrigerator, so the iceman was a daily visitor as he was at many other houses on our block. In addition to the iceman, other street vendors periodically came through our neighborhood.

The most interesting independent street vendor was the scissor-man. His job was to sharpen knives and, of course, scissors, and he also mended umbrellas. (A very versatile fellow.) About once a month he would announce his arrival by tooting a tin horn as he came down the street pushing a strange looking wooden cart that looked like a very tall wheelbarrow.

When he was stopped by a customer, he would flip the cart up and over and set it down to reveal a huge grindstone. He would then sit down on a built-in work seat and get the stone turning with a foot treadle as he put a new edge on the client's dull cutlery.

All this, of course, was done in front of a spellbound audience of little kids and even a few adults. When there was no TV to watch, the scissor-man becomes prime-time entertainment.

There also was the milkman who came by on his daily rounds before dawn. I remember seeing him going back to the dairy's nearby parking garage later in the day. Some milk routes were still served by horse-drawn wagons while others used battery-powered trucks. Our milkman drove a tall, boxy green electric truck with the dairy's name, *Wanzer*, painted in shiny gold letters on all sides.

An interesting feature about the truck's design was that there was no driver's seat for the milkman. He drove standing up. And the truck was almost silent as it hummed down the street. It's hard to imagine that this vehicular technology was readily available back then. And, after the trucks were replaced with gasoline-powered ones (or none at all when the milkman himself was eliminated), the design was somehow lost and has not been reinvented even now as the end of the millennium has come and gone.

The strangest (and rattiest) of the street vendors was not a vendor at all — he did not sell, he bought. He was, for all practical purposes, the original re-cycler. He drove a horse-drawn cart down the street or alley and bought recyclable discards such as clothing: anything metallic such as pots and pans, or even worn machinery and tools. He announced his presence in the neighborhood by chanting in a sing-song manner, "Rags-o-la-ee."

It was many years later that I finally found out what he was saying: "Rags-old-iron." (It is very difficult to say the word "iron" in a loud voice. Try it.)

Of course all of these horses going through the neighborhood produced a lot of horse crap. Large lumps of it could be seen on the street every day. The amazing thing was it never stayed in the street very long. Very soon after the steaming pile hit the asphalt, some homeowner would be out there picking it up with a shovel and depositing it into a backyard garden plot. The old "waste not, want not" habits learned in the far-off villages of Europe were hard to break, even in a new setting.

With all the horse-drawn vehicles on the streets, it was not surprising that, every now and then, an old nag would, sadly, breathe its last while on the job. I remember more than once seeing a collapsed horse, still tied to its traces, lying near the curb while its owner paced worriedly nearby wondering how he would be able to conduct tomorrow's business without his faithful, and probably overworked, "engine."

We didn't have many appliances, and among the many, many other things we did not have were a full-time, on-demand water heater. (These came into wide use much later.) In the kitchen was a flash boiler that was turned on only when hot water was needed. It was a wall-mounted, black cylinder about three-feet tall and less than a foot in diameter. Behind a curved door was a huge gas-driven burner with a coiled water pipe running through it. When hot water was required, the door was opened, a valve was turned on, the gas was lit with a wooden kitchen match and the flames heated the water as it passed through the internal coiled pipe.

A little semi-opaque isinglass window in the door showed the blue flame and also served as kind of an ON indicator. (The little window was probably unnecessary because the roar of the fire and the creaking of the heated metal could have sufficed for that purpose, to say nothing of the smell of leaking fumes.) Most of the burnt gasses were vented up through a small metal stack and out of the house via a wall-mounted connection.

In addition to the need to turn the unit on and off, there also was an important operational factor that had to be observed. When the fire was on, the water had to be in motion towards the kitchen sink or bathtub, or else a minor (or even a major) steam explosion could occur.

Unfortunately, no matter how carefully one adjusted the water's flow out of the sink/tub faucet, steam bubbles formed and pounded the pipes until they either cooled or violently escaped in a dangerous swoosh and sputter from the open faucet. As backward as this procedure seems, it was still far better than having to heat pots of water on the stove to wash clothes or take a bath.

I believe this primitive method of water heating was partially responsible for my mother's lifelong obsession with hot water and its conservation. (More on this subject later.)

While on the subject of fire and flame, there were two other instances of them in our house — the furnace and the kitchen stove.

Our furnace was in the basement. (Not all of our neighbors could make that statement, as I shall describe later.) It was a huge monster of a machine with many large round pipes emanating from its top. It looked like an inverted metallic spider holding up the house.

The furnace was coal-fired and the metal pipes ducted heated air to all of the rooms. The airflow was not assisted by a fan but simply rose upward through natural convection. Several large metal floor grates located throughout the first-floor apartment served as cold-air returns.

The second-floor apartment was not connected to the furnace. Its heat was provided by several oil-burning space heaters located throughout the apartment.

Heating oil for all burners was stored in the basement and had to be carried upstairs in large five-gallon cans and transferred into each burner's oil reservoir. Not only was this an inconvenient arrangement, but the entire operation was very dangerous. A house fire could occur at almost any step along the way.

Getting back to the furnace: it was hand-fired by shovel from a coal bin located nearby in the basement. The coal bin had a wall-mounted access door that opened onto the side of the house into the narrow gangway. Coal was delivered by either horse-drawn wagon (small load) or via truck (probably a chain-driven Reo, the most popular truck of its time). In either case, since the bins were small, several coal deliveries were necessary during the winter months.

Because there was no direct access to the coal bin from the front of the house, it couldn't simply be sent down a shoot. The delivery guy had to move the entire load with a shovel and a wheelbarrow — a very hard and dirty job.

The coal usually came in large chunks, some almost as big as a basketball. (I believe it was cheaper that way because it required less processing.) It was shiny black and smelled faintly of sulfur. The biggest coal lumps had to be broken up with a hammer, which fortunately was easy to do as coal is very brittle. These manageable pieces were then carried on a shovel to the furnace to stoke the fire.

With everyone burning this cheap, soft coal, Chicago's winter sky turned a smoky gray, a color I would not see anywhere again until I moved many years later to the smog of Los Angeles.

Shoveling the coal into the furnace was the easy part. What was harder and messier was the removal of ashes and clinkers. (A clinker is the mass of non-burnable coal residue that has melted together and fused into a gnarly clump that looks almost metallic, but is very light.) These had to be removed along with the ashes.

Ash removal was simple because it could be shaken down through grates. Clinker removal was a daily chore which was further complicated by the fact that it could only be done when the furnace had very little or no fire inside. This operation had to be performed quickly because, if the furnace was cold, it also was cold upstairs.

Following clinker removal, a new fire had to be started. To add to the complexity of the entire operation, the furnace fire also had to be properly banked before the family went to bed, or else it would go out during the night. If that happened, the Chicago winter would be free to quickly enter the house. A good supply of kindling wood was always kept on-hand next to the furnace to restart the coal fire.

None of this operation easily lent itself to automation. It was human-driven and far more complex than setting a thermostat. The temperature in the house was governed strictly by the size of the fire in the furnace. If it was too cold upstairs, more coal had to be added, usually in the middle of the night. If it got too hot, several windows or doors had to be opened until the heat wave passed. I'm almost certain that the prevailing temperatures in our house tended to be on the colder side.

In addition to the basement furnace and oil-fired space heater mentioned above, there was another variety of home-heaters that were used but were quickly losing popularity at the time. This was the coal-burner stove that was located inside the house. We did not have one, but many of my friends did.

It was not a fireplace or a fancy wood-burning stove but a huge semi-pot-bellied mass that dominated a central open space, usually between the front room and the dining room. It was made out of shiny, well-polished metal and had a large number of small windows located on its entire surface. (These windows were not unlike the peephole found on the flash burner.) The stove had huge metal feet that stood on a fireproof metal mat (a good thing!) that also was the resting place for a coal bucket or coal scuttle.

A fire was continuously maintained inside the stove just like in a furnace. And, also like a furnace, resultant ashes and clinkers had to be dealt with regularly. It's hard enough to imagine how the inherently dirty clinker/ash removal operation could successfully be performed in the basement much less inside the living quarters of an apartment. It is also hard to imagine how toddlers could be kept away from the stove, or how the residents kept from accidentally bumping into it while simply moving around the not-so-large apartment. People who had these stoves could identify each other by the ugly burn scars on their elbows.

Because it had no ductwork, the stove supplied heat by radiation. The only way to heat a room far away from the stove was to heat — and I do mean HEAT — all of the rooms in between. On really cold days, the stove would be fed so much fuel that portions of the surface would glow a deep cherry red, but to no avail. The rooms furthest away would still be cold.

Our first kitchen stove was a cast iron, wood-fired unit. The design of these stoves had been perfected over time and they worked very well. They were practically air-tight, so they had a terrific draft. Very little smoke escaped into the house. Of course, their use required a considerable amount of planning because the warm-up period was substantial.

After a couple of years, the woodstove was replaced by a natural gas model, and a refrigerator was added to our meager list of modern appliances.

Even though the quality of the kitchen equipment improved, the dinner menu remained about the same. The family continued to eat meals that were only slight variations of a Polish peasant's diet. Mostly we had boiled chicken, fried meats, potatoes, beets, and cabbage as repetitive staples. These were prepared in the simplest manner using salt and pepper as our only known spices.

However, some traditional Polish dishes found their way to the table with slight modifications or even improvements to the original, old country recipes.

Golabki, for instance, had tomato sauce added which was an ingredient not readily available in Poland.

One major item missing from our diet was corn in any form. Back in the home village, corn was considered to be food that was only fit for pigs and was avoided completely. Only the really poor people in the village would resort to eating it, and only in a disguised state. The lowest, most demeaning form was to eat corn-on-the-cob.

Eating corn directly off of the cob was tantamount to admitting total financial defeat. I wonder what my parents thought when they saw billboard ads featuring happy kids eating corn. The scene must have presented mixed signals.

Fresh fruit was seldom available, but we did have plenty of dried prunes and occasionally, some canned fruit cocktail. The only cheese we ever ate was in the form of cottage cheese, and we never had salad. In fact, the first salad I had was when I ordered one in a restaurant as a young adult. A simple food like dry cereal was also unknown in our house. I remember hearing about *Kellogg's Pep* on the *Adventures of Superman* radio show, but I had no idea what they were talking about until I finally bought some myself.

At first, my mother did laundry by-hand in a tub with a washboard. This must have been quite laborious with a small infant in the house requiring cloth diaper changing almost continuously. For this reason, the kids in my generation were subjected to early and intense toilet training — with life-long consequences, I might add.

Before hanging the wet laundry out on a clothesline, each piece was run through a hand-cranked wringer to remove most of the water. For a while, I helped with the clothes-wringing process because it was a new and exciting thing to do. As with any kid, however, the novelty soon wore off and it became a chore instead of eager fun.

I remember being a young Gutenberg of printing-press fame when I discovered that a sheet of newspaper would leave a reverse image on a damp roller. This printing could then be faintly transferred to a clean piece of paper. This experiment, although mildly successful, ended in me getting beaten because the inked image transferred onto just-washed clothes as well.

For some reason, my mother held onto all of these vintage laundry tools even after they had purchased an electric washing machine. I recovered some of them from her basement and still have them at this writing.

I remember none of the tenant families we had, except one. They lived upstairs on Kamerling Avenue and had a son and daughter, both much older than I. The son had been drafted into the Army along with all other eligible 18-year olds.

I was just about six years old at the time when Allied forces landed in North Africa, one of the early U.S. actions of World War II. A few days after the start of the campaign, the Western Union telegram delivery man showed up with the dreaded "I regret" telegram from the War Department.

I remember how the mother wailed when she answered the door and refused to take the brown, windowed-envelope, hoping that this act of denial would somehow bring her dead son back. His parents probably never visited his grave in that far-off U.S. Army cemetery in Libya.

I also remember another incident that occurred when the war finally ended. By that time, we had moved to Crystal Street and I had a new friend named Tommy. (His most distinguishing and, it turns out, most memorable characteristic was that the family was Lutheran. Oh, oh!)

Tom and I were playing in his house one day when his father — who had served in the Army during the war — just walked right in! He was still in his green uniform with a duffel bag slung over his shoulder, looking like a V-for-Victory poster boy.

Tom and his mother screamed and ran to hug him — and so did I. It clearly seemed like the thing to do, even though I had never seen the man before.

———

PERSPECTIVE: I guess I lived through some hard times, but then again, being a kid is always hard. However, starting life on a disadvantaged level does have one good aspect: things can only get better — and for me, they did.

2

Early Years

Chances are I probably was not a very good kid — or that's what my mother told me almost continuously. Every other kid she knew was better behaved and a lot smarter in school (probably taller and better looking, too). I believed all of this to be true until I witnessed how some of the so-called better kids in my grade school class acted and how they got treated in their own homes. They did about the same stupid things I did and often paid the same price. When I tried to relate this phenomenon to my mother, I got accused of lying, so I just stopped talking about it.

I do know one thing for sure: I was a lot more logical than many of my peers and, certainly, more so than my mother. I particularly remember being chastised for some infraction or other and being told that; because I was bad to my parents, my children would be bad to me. When I asked if all parents who have bad children were themselves bad, I was told "yes." I then stated the obvious: since I was bad to my parents, it is therefore logical that my mother must also have been bad as a child.

I never heard that proverb mentioned again. The illogic of it all caused me to question, or at least examine, the other so-called universal truths to which I was being exposed.

A prime example of proverb-busting was my response to my mother's statement that "a person cannot cut bread unless he has earned it." By this she simply meant that a person could not respect what he hasn't worked for. In this particular case, he will do a sloppy job of cutting the bread he hasn't earned. There probably was some truth to this statement, but I did not see how it could be a hard-and-fast rule.

Sliced bread had not been invented yet, so even *Wonder* Bread was packaged and sold in one piece as a loaf. You had to cut it yourself. As a little kid I tried to cut bread and, of course, made a jagged, torn mess of it. When I heard the "earn/cut" proverb, I resolved to disprove it. The next chance I got, I cut very slowly and carefully and succeeded: I cut off a smooth slice and proved it could be done by someone who actually didn't have a job. This great feat was dismissed by my mother as an anomaly. One to be ignored.

This event did have a lasting impression on me, however. Now, whenever I cut into a loaf of un-sliced bread, I often stop to admire the straight lines of each slice and I think about the determination of that little kid a long time ago. I also wonder why a smart-ass five year-old was allowed to play with a large kitchen knife.

This tendency for myth busting did not cease as I got older. For example, one of the concepts that all ten year-olds held to be absolutely true was: if you drop dry ice into water, the result is poisonous.

This belief was based upon the obvious violence one could see as the dry ice melted. That violent reaction could only spell poison. Well, I didn't believe it because I had read somewhere that what was produced was carbonated water — the main ingredient in *Coke* and *Pepsi* and also *Royal Crown Cola,* my favorite.

Quite often my friends and I would beg small samples of dry ice from the *Good Humor* man and then drop these samples into water to watch them fume and buzz around. On one such occasion I announced it was possible to drink the water after the dry ice stopped fizzing and suffer no negative effects. This brought a gasp from the assembled and immediately resulted in a challenge to "Prove it. I dare yah."

I accepted the challenge and said I would drink the half-filled contents of a *Pepsi* bottle after the dry ice chip had done its work. The word quickly got out that I was going to poison myself on purpose and a minor crowd of urchins gathered to bear witness to the event.

I sat facing the crowd, which watched breathlessly as I lifted the bottle and drank. It tasted horrible but I had to finish it to prove my point. As I drank the last of the "Hemlock," I looked down to see their disappointment. They wanted to witness a suicide and all they saw was somebody drinking fizzy water. I understood fully because I too would have been equally disappointed if I had been in the crowd.

Disciplinary ideas were different then and parents behaved in ways that would be totally unacceptable today — at least mine did. Since I was, by definition, not a well-mannered kid, I was beaten a lot. Razor strap, sticks, open or closed fists. Whatever was handy. Apparently these punishments were not too severe, because I continued to do whatever it was that justified the beatings in the first place.

Sometimes while being hit I would unconsciously raise my arms to defend myself. This natural reaction was interpreted as "how dare you raise your fist to hit your mother" which only extended the beating interval. The first time I did this I was told, "If you hit your mother, your arm will stick out of the grave after you're dead and buried." (Honestly, where did she get this stuff?)

When I heard this, I was horrified! What a gruesome concept! The next time we went to the cemetery, I looked around for a show of hands sticking out of the ground. I wanted to see the boney arms with tatters of rotting cloth blowing in the wind as depicted on horror comic book covers. To my disappointment, there were none. Surely some of these people must have been mother-beaters. When I relayed this observation to my mother, I received that disappointed "little-proverb-destroyer" look that I soon began to relish.

Another incident that demonstrates the clashing of not only generations but educational levels comes to mind. When we started studying geography in school, I came home and announced that the state of Texas was larger than all of Poland (which is true). My mother immediately challenged this remark and, to prove it, pointed to two maps mounted on the wall: one of Poland and the other of the United States. "Anyone can see," she said, "that Poland is not only larger than Texas, but it's also larger than the entire United States."

When I tried to explain the concept of map scale, she would have none of it. And so it ended because I didn't want to risk the usual consequences of mouthing off.

At about the age of ten, electricity became a fascination when I discovered I could light a flashlight bulb with a battery and two pieces of wire. I began to experiment with simple circuits and soon invented the telegraph,[3] the electro-magnet, and the buzzer. Most of these were crude assemblies that used household items and *Erector Set* parts, but they worked nonetheless. I was on my way to electrical greatness.

As a result of these early experiments, I soon developed my own theory on how electricity works. I assumed that something flowed out of the positive battery terminal and something else flowed out of the negative terminal. Then, when these two unknown some things met in the middle (inside a light bulb, for example) they would annihilate each other and thereby produce light. Of course none this is true as I later found out, but if this principle is carefully followed, a simple electric circuit can be constructed.

I quickly became bored of battery-driven circuits. I wanted to deal with more power, so I then began working with house wiring. When our house was built, both apartments were originally equipped with gas-lighting. These were replaced years later with electric lights that hung in the center of each room's ceiling. These lamps were all controlled by pull-chains and my mother wanted the "modern look" of wall switches.

At the ripe old age of eleven I figured out how this could be done and got the job of re-wiring not only our apartment, but those of our tenants and even at my stepfather Alex's properties. In addition to installing wall switches, I also added wall outlets. This actually made the house safer by eliminating many of the extension cords

---

3 Clearly, Sam Morse and others beat me to it by more than 100 years, but I did not know that.

previously used to power radios, irons and the growing list of home electrical appliances.

At first this was fun, but then it soon became just another one of my jobs.

My wiring fame soon spread and I even got a few outside rewiring jobs from some of my mother's lady friends in the neighborhood. I liked these jobs because I got paid real money for them. I might add that all of these wiring upgrades were successful, and none resulted in a fire or damage of any kind. Or, if there were any, I never heard of any resulting problems.

My mother was a firm believer in diaries. She referred to them as her "history" and recorded events from her life in numerous notebooks and even on loose scraps of paper which she taped and stuffed into the more formal ledgers.

In the late 1980s I found a few of these diaries when we moved her things into our house. They are all in Polish, of course, and many of them date back to the 1920s when my parents were first married. I suspect that they may contain some real insight into her feelings about Edward's illness, his death and even about my birth and early life. There is probably a lot I can learn from them, and someday I may task myself to translate them, but right now, I just don't feel the need to do so.

I also found some of my own early writings mixed in among my mother's journals. One diary was written during my first summer vacation from high school when I was about 14 years old. For some reason, I wrote it in Polish. Why, I don't know. I suspect that my mother insisted that I keep a record of my activities and she wanted to be able to read it to keep tabs on me. She probably figured that I was stupid enough to record all of my transgressions so that I would incriminate myself.

During summer vacation when I was nine, while heading home in the dark, I took a short cut through our corner prairie and tripped on something. I tried to break my fall by sticking out my arms but landed on the right palm with too much force and jammed my elbow out of joint. I remember completing the trip home wondering why my right arm was noticeably shorter than the left.

I showed this to my father who grabbed my wrist and pulled the elbow back into place. This felt better, but only in contrast and only for a short while. The next day after a miserably painful and feverish night my mother and I took the streetcar to see the doctor — the very same one who was present at my birth.

He took me into his X-ray room and laid my elbow on the table. As he moved the camera into position, I looked up and saw this huge, black machine moving menacingly closer to my arm. I had never seen an X-ray machine so I had no idea what was going to happen next. I assumed he was going to press it down on my elbow and this was, somehow, part of the curing process. I fainted.

Well, that caused a bit of unplanned commotion and anxiety for all present. But, I soon recovered and the doctoring proceeded.

X-rays were taken and a heavy plaster cast applied. This stayed on for many weeks during which time most normal street activities were not possible but were attempted anyway.

As with all casts it soon became an annoyance. Besides, it was extremely itchy during the rest of the hot Chicago summer. Some of my friends signed the cast with all sorts of writing instruments so after a few weeks, it was pretty grimy — and smelly too.

After the cast was removed it was obvious that the doctor had not examined the X-ray picture very carefully. If he had he would have noticed that the elbow joint was also heavily damaged and, after the bone fractures mended, the joint remained very stiff — almost frozen in a bent position.

I was disappointed to learn after carrying that cast around for weeks that I could not bend my arm more than a few degrees without experiencing huge pain. Of course the doctor did not feel at all responsible for this screw-up and probably blamed me for somehow messing up the healing process. (Today he could have been sued, I suppose.)

For the next few weeks I had to undergo self-applied therapy which consisted of soaking the elbow in hot water while trying to flex the joint. This proved to be a very painful and lengthy exercise. After a while I finally got my elbow working again but not completely because, to this day, I cannot touch my right shoulder.

And so I made it through early childhood with only one trip to the hospital. However, considering the large number of foolish things we did as kids, that was quite an achievement.

PERSPECTIVE: Growing up is hard to do.

3

Family

Both of my parents came from small villages in Southern Poland, in the foothills of the mountains that form part of the Polish/Czech border. As mentioned previously, these folk were known as "Gorale" or hill people — Polish hillbillies, actually. My father, John, was born in 1889 and my mother, Aleksandra, in 1900. (Her name was spelled using "ks" because the Polish alphabet does not contain an "x.") They did not know each other while living in what was known as "The Old Country" even though their homes were only a few miles apart. They met in Chicago through mutual friends and relatives.

In Poland, they were no different from all the other poor peasants, living in a semi-feudal environment. Although each family did own the property on which they worked, they did not live on the land as do farmers in this country.

Everyone lived in tiny villages, which really were no more than casual groupings of houses clustered together for protection and convenience. Of course there were no paved roads, formal markets or any amenities such as running water or electricity. I remember seeing an ancient photograph of the house where my mother was born. (Unfortunately, the photo has been misplaced.) It showed a one-room hut with a thatched-straw roof and a dirt-floor interior. I never saw a picture of my father's house, but it was probably no better.

Every day the peasants and their children would go out to work their land, most of which was located some distance from the village. These pieces of land were just that, irregularly shaped pieces. After hundreds of years of dividing the property so it could be inherited by the next genera-tion, many plots became too small to farm. Some were only a few feet wide, not much bigger than gar-den plots. The other problem was that, as time went on and the plots got smaller, they also became  more numerous. Soon each peasant family had many tiny plots of land, which were scattered all around the village. Each family there-fore required a large number of children to get all the work done. This arrangement also resulted in cutting the land into even smaller parcels for the next, even poorer generation. This is probably the main reason why Poland was not a very prosperous agrarian society.

Each small plot had a different purpose: one was used to graze the animals, another to grow kitchen vegetables and yet another for crops destined for market. Children were assigned to every plot and would remain in the field most of the day. It was their responsibility to insure the cow did not wander off and the crops were not over-grown with weeds. It was a tough life.

In addition to fulfilling the primary role of farmer, my grand-father was also a blacksmith and a wheelwright. (These were common professions at the time due to the large number of horses and wagons in use everywhere.) The shed containing his anvil, tools and hearth was set up in one corner of the family lot not too far from the thatched homestead. Alas both the shed and the ancient homestead are gone. (A picture of the site showing its simple design and even some tools and equipment is shown at the end of this chapter.)

My maternal grandmother died when my mother was about ten years old. She and her older sisters had to take care of the younger children and were responsible for all the household chores in addition to their field duties.

After his wife died, my grandfather did not remarry and lived to be ninety-eight years old. I've been told that he continued to work in the smithy shed well into his 80s. My mother certainly inherited his genes for stamina and longevity as she also lived to be ninety-eight years old.

As was the case with many of my friends who also were first-generation Americans, I never met any of my grandparents. They were either dead or lived far off in Poland. I did learn late in life that my father's father had come to the United States several times during the late 1890s, early 1900s. He would stay about a year at a time, work some menial factory or maintenance job, save all of his scrimpy pay and then return to his village. There he would be considered rich because he had money to spend, whereas everyone else in the village traded on the barter system. He probably used the funds he earned to buy adjoining plots of land from his neighbors, thereby increasing his land's meager productivity due to the benefits of scale.

I believe my father came here prepared to follow in his father's footsteps. He probably intended to stay a short time then return to his native village as a relatively prosperous man. Unfortunately, several things went wrong with his plans. Principle among them was that World War II got in the way of his return. Then, when the war was finally over, Poland came under Soviet control and was not a place where one would want to emigrate. Besides, by then he was a lot older and probably worn out, physically unable to realize the dream of being a large-scale farmer.

As part of his original great plan, he purchased a relatively huge tract (about 40 acres) of land in Poland during the 1920s. (How this transaction was completed, I do not know.) The property was located close to land already owned by his relatives, and they agreed to farm it for him pending his planned and triumphant return. Being his oldest son, I inherited this acreage after he died, but I no longer own it. I deeded it to these same unknown distant relatives in the mid-1960s. My mother hand-carried the transfer papers to her in-law family on her one and only return visit to her motherland.

I don't have many valid memories of my father, and I certainly don't remember him being sick. Parental illness was the type of information that was kept from little kids. All I know is that one morning my mother told me that my Tata (my name for my father) had died during the night at the hospital. My only question was, "Do I have to go to school today?" Incidentally, it was also my tenth birthday.

I was an instant celebrity at school for a few days and the object of pity and concern for a while thereafter. This soon wore off and I reverted to my familiar rank of class jerk, except now I was the only class jerk with a single parent. I retained the status of half-orphan for the next 50 years. (The class jerk part only partially went away.)

My brother Edward was born in 1925 and died ten years later, one year before I was born. My only involvement with him was going to visit his gravesite on Sunday afternoons with my parents, and later with just my mother. We would take the Milwaukee Avenue streetcar out to the end of the line in Niles, Illinois, and then walk about six blocks. Along much of the route were empty lots, as the area had not yet been built up.

Because there were very few passengers getting on or off, the streetcar could reach its terminal velocity along this empty stretch of track — probably about 30 miles per hour. As it rocked, swayed and rolled along, I would invariably get carsick and barf. Going to the cemetery was not much fun for me or for my parents — or for the other streetcar passengers, for that matter.

My parents each had an older sister living in Chicago. My mother's sister was named Solomeia but she was called "Solly" by all her friends. I don't remember the name of my father's sister because I called both of them "Ciocia," which is simply "Aunt" in Polish.

Both sisters had two children each, a boy and girl. All these cousins were much older than I; or so I thought at the time because of being the baby of the clan. The boys from both families were about the same age, both served in the Navy during the War, and coincidentally both returned to work for, and retire from, the United States Postal Service.

I had more interface with the family on my mother's side then with my father's relatives. When I was in high school and college, my cousin Walter (Solly's son) would use his insider's influence to get me temporary jobs delivering mail during the Christmas season.

It was while on temporary duty at the Post Office when I first witnessed government workers in operation. (I hesitate to use the term "action" in this context.) Cousin Walter, with years of experience behind him, advised me that, if ever I wanted to work for the government, I should work as hard on the first day as I planned to work on the very last day prior to retirement. That way I could never be accused of slowing down on the job. This sage advice explained why all of those 30 year old men I saw at the Post Office moved around as though they were 65 years old or older. This behavioral lesson has served me well over the years.

I remember my aunt Solomeia as a quiet, pudgy little woman who resembled the central figure in Norman Rockwell's famous painting showing the table set for a huge Thanksgiving feast. She was married to my uncle John, whom I feared. (Rockwell would never use him as a model.) He was a very somber person who resembled Joseph Stalin: without the mustache, but with the same demeanor. He ruled the family in much the same way that Joe ruled Russia; with an iron fist.

When Solomeia died accidentally in the late 1950s by falling down her basement stairs, my mother immediately suspected that she didn't fall, but was pushed by my uncle John. The incident remained an open issue from that point onward.

Solomeia's son Walter had a younger sister named Wanda. (At that time, it seems that all Polish families had kids named Walter and Wanda.) I remember her as being quiet and reclusive, probably as a result of having Uncle John as her domineering father. She never married and lived a quiet life with her special friend in the Chicago suburbs.

Contact with the other cousins almost ceased after my father died. We did meet occasionally, but it was rare. My cousin Marian (aka Mamie) married a strange little guy named Peter. Because Pete wasn't Polish, Marian's parents did not approve of the marriage. Nonetheless, after the wedding, the newly married couple moved into the first floor apartment of the two-flat that my aunt and uncle owned on the North Side of Chicago. (By the way, this moving in with the in-laws was a normal, totally acceptable mode of behavior following a Polish wedding.)

Pete seemed to be out-of-work a lot and, for some reason, didn't seem to mind that everyone in the house spoke this strange language that he didn't understand. At family gatherings, he would just sit there and smile through his highball glass while everyone else talked around him — and about him. If he knew what his in-laws were saying, he would have moved out — which is probably what they wanted in the first place. In a way, he did leave a short time later. He died under strange circumstances. It was attributed to a heart attack, but my mother, typically, suspected poison.

We had one other distant relative, probably on my mother's side, also living in this country. That family, whose name I do not know, had a farm somewhere in Northern Indiana. It must have been a large chicken farm because, during the war, they would occasionally send us several dozen eggs delivered by mail. (No doubt to help us through the rationing period.)

The eggs would arrive in a specially-constructed wood and wire container, which, if full, could hold upwards of 12 dozen eggs. The egg crate was heavily insulated from shock through use of cardboard baffles arranged between egg layers. Today if anyone considered sending eggs through the mail (even in an old egg crate) he would be labeled as crazy, but back then it seemed to work. Maybe because the container was so unique in its design that it got special treatment all along its route.

After the eggs were removed, my mother would pack some items into the empty crate such as homemade bread or maybe an issue of the Polish newspaper and send it back to her relative with a letter or thanks. I suspect all of the eggs were not consumed at home and some were probably traded with neighbors for other scarce items on the Rationing Board's list.

After my father died, my mother and I both received monthly survivor-benefit checks from Social Security. I received these checks until I turned 18 years old. (I did not see a single one and only found out about them when I was almost 30 years old.) My checks were about $20 per month, but that amount went a lot further then. The caveat was that my mother's checks would stop coming if she remarried or got a paying job, kind of how welfare payments are supposed to work today.

Because the checks were too small to live on, she needed to get a job. She applied for work at a commercial laundry located in our neighborhood while posing as her sister Solly. Her sister did not have a job at the time so my mother simply used her sister's name and Social Security number without fear of getting caught. My mother worked with this false identity for several years. How the both of them handled the income tax issue is anyone's guess.

After a year or two of widowhood, Aleksandra met and married Alexander Dmus. (Because he came from a different part of Poland, he apparently had easier access to the letter "x.") Alex was a widower and a bit older than my mother. He had two grown children, ages 34 (Helen) and 37 (Chester).

Prior to the wedding, Alex and Helen lived in a very run-down area of Chicago, about a block from the Lake Street El on Avers Avenue, right next to some railroad tracks. The neighborhood had deteriorated over time and typically, he didn't notice the advancing decay. By comparison, our house on Crystal Street was "the shnitz."

Alex was born in the late 1880s in Eastern Poland/Western Russia. At that time the border between the two countries was very fluid, so technically, he may not even have been Polish.

He spoke Russian and Polish plus a reasonable amount of English and he taught me how to count to ten in Russian — which I still remember.

When Alex was in his teens, the last Czar of Russia was in power and involved in one of his many wars. Alex was afraid of getting forcibly conscripted so, as a teenager, he ran away from home and ended up in Chicago. Soon after arriving, he managed to get a menial job at the Goodman Manufacturing Company located on the far South Side of the city. The factory made specialized machinery for use in coal mines such as ore crushers and small locomotives. He definitely was not part of the high tech industry. However, he must have been a bright lad because he soon worked his way up the chain, became a machinist and stayed with the firm for almost 50 years!

Every morning Alex got up before 5:00 am and rode several streetcars for an hour to get to work. He was always on-time. I happened to be living at home when he retired. I wondered what would happen to him when he finally did stop working. What would he do with himself? Not much, as it turned out. The first morning he slept until 9:00 am. When I asked him how he could just turn it off so quickly after all that time, he replied, "That's easy. I've always hated that place."

At work he operated a huge milling machine, and his job was to cut keyway slots into the ends of large shafts. I often could see the results of his work when he brought home some metal filings imbedded deeply into his hands and fingers. I'd help remove these metal splinters with a needle because they were too small for him to see.

To describe his hands as being leathery would be too kind. They were surprisingly small and had a smooth and extremely hard crusty surface as though they were made of one continuous callous. It was quite clear that this man did not have an office job. Every time I helped him remove splinters I would wonder if my hands would look like his in 50 years.

I don't recall being invited to his factory on 'bring-your-kid-to-work day', but I'm sure that if such an event existed, I would have turned down the opportunity. I probably saw it as being an un-cool thing to do. Too bad. It would have been interesting.

Alex and Aleksandra had a bad marriage from the start and they fought almost continuously. After each fight, my mother would tell me what a rotten person he was and I would agree with her. However, after many years of thinking about it, I have changed my viewpoint somewhat. Although I still believe Alex's behavior was wrong in many ways, I also understand that he was simply a product of his times and was not unique in his philosophy.

He and most men of his social status honestly believed the man was the supreme boss of the household and whatever money he earned belonged to him, to spend as he wished. A contribution to the family's expenses that came from his tightly-closed wallet should be considered a gift and should be acknowledged as such by all grateful family members.

If my mother knew of these beliefs prior to the wedding, she certainly acted surprised when he tried to put them into play. This major difference of opinion about money was the root cause of their many squabbles.

Alex moved into our house on Crystal Street after the wedding, but his daughter Helen stayed alone in the Avers apartment. Because she was a modern young woman, she probably did not get along with my mother and therefore preferred to live alone.

Occasionally my mother would try to get on Helen's good side and I would be ordered to take her some home-cooked food. The distance between our house and her Avers apartment was about 12 blocks and I would make the delivery on my bike,[4] carrying the food in a wire basket attached to the handlebars.

About a year after the marriage, Helen either got tired of living alone or got scared of the old neighborhood and moved in with us. She was short and cute and played the piano quite well. (Her piano moved in with her.) It was then that my mother got the idea that Helen would pay for her keep by teaching me to be a piano player.

Better she should have stayed on Avers.

---

4 The bike was an old hand-me-down I got from Helen. Not only was it a girl's bike but its tires were made of red rubber! I was open to ridicule from two directions.

Although she was not a trained piano teacher, she made up for it in kindness. She did not threaten or beat me as I expected: that was still my mother's job. Her approach was always calm and reassuring. Her efforts, however, met with total failure. I hated to practice and hated to play, and never got very far into the lesson plans. To this day I honestly regret having had such a bad attitude.

After living with us for about a year, Helen got married to a nice fellow from Poland named Ted who was a year or two younger than she. (My mother said she lied to him about her age.) While she was single, Helen managed to save a lot of money and was able to immediately buy a house in a far-off suburb called Hinsdale. (Today this is a very fancy ZIP code.)

Alex didn't like his son-in-law. He figured Ted was after Helen's money. (Everything was always about money.) Alex also didn't like the idea that Ted had somehow "forced" Helen to move so far away. (About 20 miles.) I'm sure Helen didn't mind the separation at all, and Ted probably didn't care what anyone else thought.

In less than a year after their marriage, Helen was pregnant and things were moving along very nicely. Then one night as they were coming home from a movie, a drunk driver broadsided them on the passenger side. She was killed instantly, and Ted was put into a coma for a week.

Alex visited Ted in the hospital after he recovered and, allegedly, asked Ted for a share of Helen's life insurance money. Naturally, Ted refused to pay. Alex stormed out of the hospital and, to the best of my knowledge; neither he nor Chester ever saw Ted again after his release from the hospital.

When Alex married my mother, Chester was already married to Priscilla and they lived in Oak Park, a very nice address at that time. They had no children.

Initially, both Chester and his wife would come by often to visit Alex and my mother. It soon became obvious that these visits were very hard on Priscilla. She couldn't follow the conversations (in Polish and broken English) plus she found the neighborhood scary and our apartment's condition well below her higher standards.

After she stopped visiting, Chester continued to come over, but very occasionally. Whenever he did show up, he and his dad would chat in private, (probably about Alex's difficult married life) and then he would leave shaking his head in wonderment.

Chester played tennis very well and was a minor celebrity on the amateur tennis circuit. In fact he won the Oak Park Tennis Open several times and had the trophies to prove it. He took me to the club with him a few times and even gave me several tennis lessons, which, to no one's surprise, I liked better than piano lessons.

I think I played fairly well for a kid. One thing for sure: I was the first kid on our block to hit a tennis ball with anything other than a broomstick.

Chester once gave me a bushel basket full of used tennis balls. This was a terrific gift and it kept the neighborhood kids well-stocked for a long time.

Many years later when I was close to graduating from high school, I proudly told Chester that I had been accepted into Illinois Institute of Technology (IIT), and I was going to someday become an electrical engineer. His only comment was, "You'll never make it." Just what I needed, some (step) brotherly support.

I also remember that on my first birthday following my mother's wedding, Chester gave me a pen and pencil set (probably expensive) with the initials "JD" (John Dmus) engraved on it. He had assumed that Alex was going to adopt me.

Well, he didn't, and just as well. The marriage just wasn't working out. My mother and Alex fought all the time, and I was expected to literally keep them apart and defend my mother. It was hard to do.

She would verbally abuse Alex continuously and occasionally would throw him out of the house. I'd have to call Chester to have him come by and fetch his father. Alex would be gone for a few days or even for as much as a few weeks. They would then get back together again and the predictable cycle would repeat itself.

I don't know if Alex stayed at his son's place whenever he got kicked out. Rumor had it that Alex had a girlfriend somewhere and that's where he spent his time following each eviction. Could be. I never asked, but I wouldn't be surprised if the story was true.

The root cause of their arguments was always about money. Prior to going into the marriage, each of them owned two houses, and each secretly planned to take control of the other's holdings. Neither plan succeeded.

They were both stubborn and they wasted their energies by fighting each other while trying to hold onto their hard-earned "fortunes." Had they been sensible and combined forces, they could have moved to better quarters in the near-suburbs as did many of their friends and relatives. But they didn't. Alex collected his own rents and my mother collected hers. They lived separate lives together and generously shared in their combined misery.

In the end, it turns out that my mother won a small victory. After Alex died in the mid-60s, she again became eligible to receive Social Security survivor benefits. This time the payments were based upon Alex's life-long SS contributions, which were much higher than hers.

On many occasions I would work for Alex at one of his properties. This consisted of cleaning, painting and even rewiring some apartments. In an effort to get on my good side, he became a generous employer, which I didn't mind at all. I guess he and I got along reasonably well.

He never hit me, although I may have deserved it on occasion. Once I borrowed his favorite straight razor to carve a model airplane's propeller spinner out of a solid block of balsa wood and practically ruined the razor's fine cutting edge.

Of course he got mad. He picked up his razor strop and, instead of beating me with it he patiently used it to hone a new edge on the damaged razor.

Soon afterward I tried to make it up to him by buying him an electric razor as a Christmas or birthday present. He thanked me for the gift, put it away unused and then gave it back to me as a present when I finally got old enough to need one.

About the same time I graduated from high school, Chester bought a new car and successfully convinced Alex to learn how to drive and, incidentally, to buy his 1938 Studebaker. Alex was almost 60 years old at the time and had never driven before. Chester taught Alex the rudiments of driving and, after a little practice; he applied for and got his driver's license.

I was absolutely amazed that this ancient person could actually learn something both new and complicated. I also soon became convinced that a huge amount of money must have been involved somewhere in order for Alex to get a driver's license. After all, this was Chicago, and that was the way things were done.

He proved to be a terrible driver. Part of it was that he was so short and the car was so large that he had to peer through the steering wheel to see down the road.

I hated to ride with him. He would go down the street at less than ten miles per hour and toot the horn almost continuously at anything within sight: a crossing pedestrian a block away, a running dog, someone on the sidewalk.

Beep, beep, beep. Maddening!

When asked why he used the horn so often he simply said, "so that they'll know I'm coming." No kidding.

A ride with Alex was also scary and more than a little bit dangerous. He never did get the hang of using the rear-view mirror; it just pointed any which way. If he wanted to see what was behind him, he would turn around and look while twisting the steering wheel toward the curb or into oncoming traffic.

He also wouldn't (or couldn't) make left turns. Fortunately for him, Chicago streets are laid out in a perfectly square, N-S/E-W pattern so, instead of making one left turn, he would simply drive past the intersection, make three right turns and be on his way again.

He also did not like to get lost. Whenever he had to go somewhere new for the first time, he would take a practice run a few days earlier and get all of the inevitable driving mistakes out of the way. I do believe he would have loved to have GPS available.

In spite of these precautions, he had many accidents and it was a wonder that he could keep his insurance coverage; if he ever had any. He hit many parked cars, and once he collided with the rear end of a stopped streetcar.

Another time, while heading for poker night after work, just as he passed in front of the Chicago stockyards, a steer escaped and came running down Halstead Street with a real rope-twirling cowboy on horseback in hot pursuit. Ever helpful, Alex stopped the beast by running into it head-on. He got his picture in the paper for that one. It was amazing, but none of these accidents were serious enough to get his license revoked although, in most instances, he had been drinking.

After I became legally old enough to drive, I could not get a license because Alex would not let me use the car, not even to practice. His reply was always the same whenever I asked him: "This is my car, I paid for it. If you want to drive a car, go buy one of your own."

Although we were not related, this is one trait that he passed on to me. Because, as a parent, I too did not believe in supplying our young kids with cars.

Alex was an avid gambler and would spend almost every Friday night playing poker in the back room of some Polish tavern on Milwaukee Avenue. It turns out that he was quite good at it too, because he would usually come home with other people's money and/or other valuable items.

He once won an expensive-looking Swiss watch from the Polish Consul to Chicago. After he died, I got this watch and, without recognizing its value, threw it away because it didn't work. I have since seen pictures of similar watches in newspaper and magazine ads which were placed by collectors looking to buy antique *Patek-Phillipe* watches, sometimes for thousands of dollars.

Alex had an older sister living in the Chicago area. She and her husband lived in a beautiful home in a fancy suburb. It was one of the few single-family homes I had ever visited and I thought of her and her husband as being very elegant, which I'm sure they were.

When I was a mid-teen, they had decided to retire and move to Florida. They had several cars, one of which was a gorgeous (I'm saying that now) red, late-20s Buick. It was the kind of squared-off boxy car with an externally-mounted spare tire that is often featured in *Archie Comics*. A potential hot rod if there ever was one. He came to our house just before their move and offered to give it to me. FOR FREE!

Before going any further, let me clarify one point. All of this happened in the 50s when Detroit was turning out some really sexy wheels. All guys my age were overcome by visions of us driving only Corvettes and Thunderbirds. I may have been poor, but I had these same high standards to uphold.

So, in one of those stupid acts in life that one regrets forever, I refused his offer. I told him that I couldn't take it because I couldn't afford the insurance (which was true). But who cares, a free car. What an idiot! In any case, I insulted the hell out him.

No one stepped forward to intervene and bring me to my senses, and he left our house visibly angry. I guess I wasn't that hung up on driving after all.

Alex's favorite saying was, "Don't worry, it's a long way to our 100th birthday," and he was thoroughly convinced he would make it. Well, he missed his mark by a long shot. He died happy, I think, at the age of 75. He suffered a fatal heart attack on a bus while on his way to the bank to deposit some recently-collected rent checks. His son inherited all of Alex's "fortune" and my mother got nothing except an increase in her Social Security check as his surviving widow.

Every month when the check arrived she would say a little prayer for Alex's soul, thank God for the extra money, and then add a small curse or two for the suffering Alex had caused her.

PERSPECTIVE: Turns out our family was about the same as what other kids had so I could not really tell at the time if it was normal, strange or wonderful. Also, because TV was not in wide use, a person could not make a comparison with "perfect" TV-families such as the ones seen on *Ozzie and Harriet* or *Father Knows Best*.

4

Mama

My mother was a fiercely independent, ambitious and highly-motivated person who also had great religious faith and always believed that God would take care of her no matter what. She was firmly convinced that her only limitation was that she was born a woman and not a man. Strangely enough, even with that thought in mind, she was a feminist long before it was acceptable or even fashionable.

She had one major flaw that simultaneously saved and doomed her: she could not detect distinctions or variations among things, places or even people. To her there was absolutely no difference between a nice house and a not-so-nice house, an old car and a new one, or clean clothes and ratty ones. They were simply "a house," "a car," or "clothes." Dirty/clean, old/new, messy/neat — all the same.

This inability to process descriptive adjectives made her life a little easier while, at the same time, drove others nuts. No amount of arguing could convince her that she was in the wrong. It also explained why she remained in a crappy Chicago neighborhood that continued to deteriorate at a phenomenal rate. She just didn't notice the downward slide.

She had a bit more formal schooling than my father, but not much more. She was allowed to attend school up to the fourth grade. Even though her formal education was lacking, she could read and write quite well, although not always grammatically correct. While I was away at school and also later after we left Chicago, she would often send me long letters written in Polish wherein she neglected to make use of a single period or comma for pages on end. The ideas in her letters just flowed, one to the next in a free-association manner.

Even though she lived in the U.S. for more than 75 years, my mother did not learn to speak English. Oh, she knew a few hundred mispronounced words that came in handy once in a while, but that was it. When in a bind, she simply made up some English words by distorting Polish ones, but that often lead to further confuse the listener.

Also, some of the English words she knew and used often were actually wrong. The best example of this was her insistence on calling a hardware store a "harvey" store. Sounds kind of close, and after a while (if you're lucky) you could figure out what she meant from the context; "I go to harvey store." It takes a little effort.

Her small village (Maszkienice) in Southern Poland was arranged in a linear fashion along both sides of a small creek, a tributary to the river Wisla. The creek served as a dividing line between villagers and it was where everyone drew their water. The lot where the combination living quarters and barn stood was very narrow — about 100 feet wide, but was very long. This odd shape resulted when the original, much larger parcel was progressively cut-up many times as each past generation divided the land among their children.

During WWI the German army set up a large military camp nearby, a portion of which was on my grandfather's property. This presented a huge burden to the family because now what little land they had was occupied by tents and military equipment and could not be farmed. Plus, they had to be extra careful with their actions and movements because the enemy was essentially located next door. All foodstuffs had to be hidden from the marauding soldiers who felt they could come and take whatever they wanted. Based upon the fragmented stories she told me when her mind was failing in the end, I believe she may have been sexually assaulted by her enemy neighbors.

Her older sister Solomea somehow managed to leave home prior to the war and settled in Chicago. She and her husband saved some money and, after the war, they sent it to Poland so that other siblings could emigrate.

My mother jumped at the chance to leave and set off on her journey via horse cart, train and finally a boat that took her to Ellis Island and the U.S. (Her exact route is unknown, but had to include crossing large portions of Poland and Germany on the way to the departure port on the Baltic Sea — most probably Bremen near Hamburg.)

Being a landlady was the source of her greatest happiness. Watching over and maintaining her six-flat apartment house (her real-estate "fortune") was all she wanted to do. It also made her very happy to do physical work. And that was a good thing considering the advanced age of the apartment building.

Even when she was well into her 80s she would work for months refinishing all of the woodwork in one of the apartments while it sat empty and unrented. Then when it was almost finished (finished/ not finished, what's the difference?) she would rent it out for a ridiculously low rent and start all over again on another apartment that had been trashed in the meantime by its recently-departed tenant.

In fact, she prized hard physical work above all other activities. To her, any form of work was a gift from God. "Every task is profitable" was one of her favorite sayings. And she really believed this even though everyone else could see that the job she was tackling was foolish and a total waste of time, money and energy.

With this narrow philosophy to guide her, it was easy to understand why she considered the use of labor-saving devices that could help finish the job sooner to be totally unnecessary. A prime example of this was when she labeled the newly-introduced paint roller as a "tool of the devil." She would rather continue using her collection of hard, stubby paint brushes which she found in the alley.

Her own apartment was a mess. It was just a warehouse for furniture, tools and bundles of rags.[5] She often referred to the place as her museum and called this assortment of old things scattered about her "antikee" but, of course, they weren't antiques at all. It was all just old junk.

---

5 In her village in Poland, cloth was not readily available and was highly treasured. Consequently, she grew up believing that it was very valuable, so she saved every piece of cloth or rag she could find.

The place was so over-crowded that movement around the apartment was limited to only a few defined pathways in a waist-high maze. The many odd furniture pieces stored there were accumulated over time when tenants moved out (usually during the night) and left many of their things behind. All of the ancient tools she used for her remodeling projects also had to be stored in her apartment because many of her tenants were petty thieves and would steal anything left in the common basement.

The collection of rag bundles was being saved because they were going to be converted into fashionable clothes someday. But they never were. Their numbers just accumulated while she walked around in truly a rag-a-muffin fashion. (She just didn't see the difference.)

When I cleaned out her apartment after she moved in with us in 1989, the accumulated trash filled an entire dumpster. Due to the massive volume involved, I could not go through and examine every object. I'm sure that not everything that was thrown out was junk.

The walls of her apartment were covered with layers of pictures of people or things which she found to be interesting. This wall art did not include photos or paintings. It consisted mostly of just pages torn out of magazines, jagged edges and all. These works-of-art were then taped onto any wall wherever there was room, and there they'd remained, often at odd angles, for years. Finally, the Scotch Tape would turn crisp and let go after which the artwork would lie decorating the floor for a while before it was replaced by a page out of a more recent issue of *Parade* magazine.

There was always a picture of the current president, a Pope or two, last year's religious calendar, grandchildren's pictures from infancy through high school and any number of flower or country scenes. Each room had its own theme-less collection. To add to this decorative artwork, she would periodically forage through the alley and bring home treasures she found among other people's trash. (Obviously an inheritable trait.)

Her eating habits were equally eclectic. Because she lived alone for many years she did not observe traditional mealtime hours but simply ate a snack whenever she was hungry. Most of her meals were consumed in a casual, grazing fashion: while standing, or while passing through the kitchen bound for her next job.

Because she lived alone her diet was totally lacking in variety. If she cooked a chicken, then that's what she ate at every meal from then on until it was gone. After the chicken was eaten, some other major food group would be introduced and totally consumed in a similar serial fashion. No food was ever thrown out. The distant memories of empty plates in Poland were just too deeply imbedded to disappear.

One other noteworthy item about the preparation of food and drink comes to mind, and that involves its temperature. Nothing that was ever eaten or drunk was either too hot or too cold, and body temperature was preferred.[6] She never, ever had an ice cube in a drink, and a room temperature Highball was considered perfect.

In spite of living under what most would see as deprived conditions, my mother was usually in good spirits. She loved to sing. Every occasion, formal or casual, would trigger a memory which

---

6 In a way, this actually makes sense. Why shock your system with very hot or very cold items?

would be greeted by a song that had some minor relationship to the event. Almost all of her songs were from her youth and most of them were either old drinking songs or plain downright bawdy. These were good for a laugh, but not after you've heard them too many times.

An interesting twist to the Polish language is that there is no formal word for "spend," as in to spend money. The closest one can come is the word "tracic" which means to waste or to lose. (Now, if that doesn't say a lot about the Poles, I don't know what else does.) Needless to say, my mother did not like to "tracic" anything, especially money. She saved everything she could, mostly through deprivation. She believed that not spending was the same as saving, which, in fact, it is. She lived simply and acted as though she was still back in her Polish village.

However, she wasn't a total shut-in and did participate in many group activities. She belonged to several Polish social clubs and loved to attend bingos and church bazaars. She also wasn't afraid to try new things as long as they didn't cost too much.

Soon after Alex learned how to drive, my mother figured if he could do it, driving must not be that hard to learn. She announced that she wanted to get a driver's license also. One day while Alex was at work, she arranged for an acquaintance to give her a driving lesson. After he explained the unfamiliar functions of the three pedals, the gearshift and the steering wheel, she decided that there were far too many items for her to handle all at once. It was then agreed that she would steer and work the brake and clutch pedals while her "instructor" operated the gas pedal and did the shifting, a script for certain disaster.

They started off in front of the house and somehow managed the first turn at the corner. But, while trying to turn again into the alley, the car lurched forward. Gas was applied, but the brakes were not. Worst of all, the steering wheel was not returned to center and the car continued to turn right. It didn't have far to go before crashing through the wall of a neighbor's garage. Thus ended the first and last driving lesson she ever had.

She always tried to save money every way she could. Since she had already cut back or eliminated all normal expenses such as food, entertainment and clothing, all she had left were utility bills. Her apartment was always dark and cold because that kept the bills down. She even saved on water bills by not bathing or washing her clothes.

There were, however, a few factors she could not fully control, such as the actions of her tenants. (There was only one water bill for the entire apartment building and she had to pay it every month.) Her tenants probably used as much water as most other people but, to my mother, the amount was always much too high, and she nagged them continuously about their wasteful ways.

What really drove her nuts was their extravagant use of hot water which was included as part of the meager rent payment. To offset this massive waste, she had a plumber install a small stove in the basement. This miniature, four-foot tall stove had a water jacket around its firebox that was connected to the inlet of the building's gas water heater.

The concept was simple: a fire in the stove would pre-heat the cold water before it entered the water heater and less gas would be required to bring it up to hot-water temperatures. In practice, it was not that simple. Since the water could only be heated when it was moving through the little stove, the only time the installation really did anything useful was when hot water was being drawn from the water heater by a tenant. Because many tenants were gone most of the day, there was no one home to use hot water and make the system pay off.

This simple plumbing fact did not dissuade my mother. Everyday — summer or winter — she would be down there stoking that little stove and heating that little bit of stagnant water and "saving money."

In itself, this little activity did no harm. It gave her something to do and it did keep the basement warm. The real problem was the way she kept the fire going. The stove's firebox was quite small because it was designed to be a garbage burner[7] and therefore was only about a foot deep. This shallow chamber did not prevent her from burning pieces of scrap lumber she had rescued from the alley. Some of these lumber pieces were often more than six-feet in length. She just propped up the exposed end of the wood as it stuck out of the stove's open door. Then she would go off to mind some other chore.

Periodically, the end of the board that was in the firebox would burn off, fall out of the stove and lie there with one end burning

---

7 An environmentally abhorrent concept when viewed today.

next to nearby wood scraps and kindling! No problem. My mother would (eventually) smell the smoke, come down and re-insert the smoldering two-by-four. Why the entire building didn't burn down continues to be a mystery.

Another mystery about my mother involved her relationship with her family in Poland. The village she left in the 1920s remained a primitive place for quite a while after WWII. Eventually, a semi-modern infrastructure consisting of electricity, sewers, running water and phones was installed. For some unknown reason, the availability of these improvements did not sit well with my mother. Their very existence actually made her angry. She apparently wanted the status quo to be maintained forever because, I think, that would justify her leaving in the first place. As long as life in the U.S. was easier and better than in Poland, she could rationalize abandoning her home, family and village. But, if Poland had the same conveniences as in the U.S., then she had no excuse for having left in the first place.

Even though she had a younger sister living in Poland, and they both had phones, she never called her. Not even once. I still don't understand why. Maybe it was the cost of a call, but I really believe she just could not bring herself to acknowledge the very existence of that phone at the other end of the line.

It turns out my mother also must have been jealous of her sister and her in-laws. When I was in eighth grade, both of these families sold their Chicago homes and moved to the nearby western suburbs. There they each bought relatively modern, four-flat apartment buildings and moved in. These moves and upgrades must have bothered my mother to the point wherein she had to somehow compete.

To do so, the following year she sold both the Kamerling and Crystal Street houses and bought a six-flat apartment building located on Karlov near North Avenue.

This was a big mistake. Instead of moving out of the city to a nicer area to the west and south, she moved further into the city to the east and north. Sure she now owned a larger building but it was located in a worst area.

All of this happened when I was away at school and could not object. Even as a teenager, I knew better. What made the situation worst for me was we had to initially move into one of the smaller, one-bedroom apartments which was vacant at the time of the sale. I therefore lost my own Crystal Street bedroom and had to sleep on the couch when I came home for school breaks. I didn't like that at all.

She lived on Karlov for almost 40 years, during which time the neighborhood deteriorated even further. To her mind, however, being the all-powerful landlady of a larger building made up for its lesser location.

Because she was quick to give advice and vent complaints, she was not on good terms with many neighbors or tenants. One night someone harboring a motive set fire to the wooden back porch and four apartments that had access to the porch were partially damaged. She was always a sound sleeper and had to be awakened and physically pulled out by the firemen.

Insurance covered the repairs but the affected apartments remained empty for several months. This experience of being rescued from of a burning building left a mark on her. She was afraid of fire from then on. When she lived with us, she would leave the room whenever we would start a fire in our fireplace.

When my wife and I got married my mother thought that we would move into one of the vacant apartments in her building — and live rent-free, by the way. In fact, she was so sure that this would happen that she fixed one of them up and kept it vacant for months before the wedding in anticipation of our moving in.

And why shouldn't she have expected this to take place? That is exactly what happened to all her friends when their sons got married. Two of my cousins moved into their parents' apartment buildings and lived there long enough to inherit the properties. In fact it was the normal rule of behavior at the time and not the exception.

I suspect she was greatly disappointed when I announced weeks before the wedding that we had rented a small apartment several miles away. Another reason for being upset was that she was absolutely sure she would became the subject of nasty talk among her friends as they all hypothesized why her only son "ran away."

Even though I was still basically a kid, I knew with absolute certainty that, if we had moved into one of her apartments, we would be stuck there forever. I would be expected to instantly respond to her demands for help around the building and we would have to answer to her for every dollar we miss-spent. Furthermore, we could never be able to leave Chicago and move to California where I could be closer to the emerging world of electronics. Fortunately for her, the embarrassment we caused among her friends did not last long. In less than six months I got a job offer to move to Los Angeles and we left the city, never to return.

During the ensuing twenty-five years, my job took our family to many other places. Meanwhile, my mother remained steadfast in her belief that we would someday return to Chicago and maybe finally move into that apartment. (Fortunately for her, she did not keep it vacant all that time.)

As stated before, she did not recognize or acknowledge that the neighborhood was deteriorating or that it was actually dangerous for her to remain there. I would call her every few weeks and we'd visit annually. However, when we came to Chicago we'd stay with my wife's parents or with her sister, never with my mother. We would only stop by and visit with her for a few hours at a time and then escape to a nicer setting.

I dreaded going there and, quite frankly, was embarrassed to be associated with that environment. (Our kids didn't mind going there when they were little, but began to object as they got older and were able to make value judgments.)

Years later when we had settled into what we thought was a "permanent" location in Maryland, we designed and built a large house in the country outside of Washington DC. With the full knowledge that my mother would someday be moving in, we included a separate three-room suite to serve as her apartment. It didn't take too long after the house construction was completed before the dreaded phone call came from Chicago — she had been hospitalized with a mild stroke.

I immediately went to visit her in the hospital. Fortunately, the stroke only affected her speech, and its effects lasted only for a few days. Meanwhile I stayed in her apartment while I packed some of her belongings and made arrangements for a nearby real estate company to take charge of the building.

Those were terribly difficult days for me. A huge number of decisions had to be made in a very short time and I had to make them all myself. But, that's the disadvantage of being an only child. I packed up a small collection of my mother's clothes in a ratty suitcase I found in the basement and we flew to her new home.

I believe she liked living with us in Maryland even though she did not fully understand where she was. We had a huge vegetable garden in which she puttered around and basically kept herself busy writing letters and reading her Polish newspaper. (I made arrangements for the paper to be mailed daily from Chicago.)

By some measures, her life ended poorly. By other standards, not bad at all.

After living with us in Maryland for five years,[8] the effects of Parkinson's became more and more evident. She lost control of her memory and many of her muscles atrophied. Walking became very difficult and writing an impossibility. In spite of the personal guarantee she had from God that she would not go to a nursing home, that's where she ended up. Saint Joseph's Home in Chicago is an old Catholic nursing home run by Polish nuns. Her final days were spent there among her own.

She survived all of her sisters and brothers, and died in November of 1998, two days short of her 98th birthday. She is buried

8 Those five years seemed so much longer at the time, but now, long after she's gone, I have a hard time remembering many details from that period. Her presence must have been very traumatic for me so I simply forgot most of it.

in Chicago at Saint Adelbert's Cemetery. The graves of my Tata and my brother Edward are there also.

Years later when my wife and I visited her birthplace in Poland I made it a point to collect a few hands-full of soil from the family garden. Then later, on a trip to Chicago, I sprinkled the dirt on her grave. I think she would have liked that. It was probably one of the few nice things I ever did for my mother.

It was during that trip to the cemetery that I learned there had been a mix-up in her burial. Instead of being interred alongside my father in the double plot she bought when he died, the cemetery management looked up the wrong Marszalek in the cemetery records and placed my mother's final resting place with my brother Edward. At first I was a bit upset, until I realized that she'd be okay with the arrangement because I knew she always liked him best.

PERSPECTIVE: My mother was very hard to live with and so was I. We were separated by so many factors that I see no need to list any of them. I often wonder if Edward had the same problems with her, although I honestly feel he did not. It's funny how they got together in the end.

5

Tata

I don't remember much about my father, John Peter Marszalek, the man I called Tata. I believe he was a quiet sort of guy who seemed to be worried a lot. All of his surviving photos show him to be a somber person. Was he worried about his health, or the family's lack of money, or about the future? I don't know.

My mother used to describe him as being a "Giant of a man. Over six-feet tall." His Polish passport tells a different story. His height is listed at five and a half feet. Who are you going to believe? (Maybe he grew after he arrived in the U.S.)

My father grew up on a farm in a small village near the town of Tarnow in the Southern part of Poland. He was among the oldest of 13 children. He received only two or three years of formal schooling because his help was needed around the house and farm. We can only try to imagine what a poorly equipped facility the schoolhouse must have been and how little knowledge was actually transferred to the kids. Consequently, he was only able to slowly read the Polish daily newspaper and could haltingly write his name. I remember sitting at the kitchen table watching him laboriously sign his name to some document and wondering what was taking him so long.

I suppose my father was a typical male immigrant in that he was more or less satisfied with just being in this country and glad he did not have to work those long hours in the dusty fields he left behind. At the same time, he probably missed his family and often thought about the good times he had when he was a kid back home. I'm sure he was also painfully aware that he could never "make it big" in this country. He and others like him were hampered by the lack of both a decent education and proper social connections. These factors combined to make him totally unequipped for success.

On the other hand, the wives of many immigrants did not understand why they had to continue to live so poorly. Why couldn't they have some of the luxuries they saw when they went downtown to clean offices at night? Many ambitious immigrant women knew that they themselves could not acquire wealth, but they just did not understand why their husbands were so inadequate to the task.

Why could they not succeed financially?

This mismatch between inflated ambition and stark reality often became a source of dispute within many immigrant families. Considering my mother's nature, I am sure it came up often in our house, too.

But, my father did not do too badly considering the small basket of skills he did have. Even though he probably never made much more than 25 cents an hour, he somehow managed to buy several rental houses, some farm property in Poland, and even dabbled in second and third mortgages just before the Depression.

My father never owned an automobile nor even sat behind the wheel of one. This was not unusual at the time. There were very few cars in our neighborhood. Most people living in Chicago, or any other large city for that matter, relied totally upon public transportation.

Fortunately, you could travel anywhere in the city by using public transport. Not only was it everywhere, it also was much more dependable and far cheaper than it is today. Streetcars were my father's only mode of going to work, visiting relatives or going to the cemetery. Everywhere else, he walked.

I remember several times my father and I went on excursions of sorts. We ventured to the far South Side of Chicago where he took me to Brookfield zoo and also to watch airplanes landing and taking off from Midway Airport. All of these trips, of course, were made on public transport.

I have no idea how he really felt about me personally. After all, I was the replacement child for his first-born son (who was, by definition, perfect) and I suspect that I just never measured up to his expectations. Was I a welcome replacement or an accidental one? I will never know.

The times must have been very difficult for him. There he was, almost 50 years old, living in a strange land, with a very uncertain world situation, poor job prospects and now, a screaming kid in the house. No wonder he worried a lot. It was probably just too much for him to bear. He probably wanted to go back to Poland, and live the good, simple life on the land he bought.

It just wasn't going to happen.

It is quite possible that my father never intended to stay in this country for the rest of his life. He may have only wanted to stay for a short time; just long enough to make some money and go back to his village. If that was his plan then he would indeed be following in his father's footsteps.

My mother told me that my grandfather came to the U.S. several times in the late 1800s as a young man, worked hard, saved his money and then went back to his village a relatively wealthy person. If this was my father's intent then too many negative things happened in the early 1900s that ruined his plan completely.

My poor Tata was relatively young when he died, less than 60 years old. I wonder how the cancer got started. Was it because of his diet? Or was it his smoking? Or maybe even the polluted industrial environments in which he worked. All these things probably contributed.

As with most smokers at the time, my father rolled his own cigarettes. His tobacco brand of choice was Bull Durham, which came packaged in a tiny cloth bag with blue drawstring closures and a small supply of cigarette paper. I do remember being sent to the nearby drug store to buy some for him. (It's hard to Imagine, but in those days a six-year-old kid was able to buy tobacco!)

I was ten years old when he died, and although it's hard to admit, I don't remember being overly sad. Was it because he was a stranger to me all along or that I just didn't appreciate the concept of death at the time? I suspect it was a little of both.

It's tough for a young boy to lose his father. His father is supposed to be his guide; always there; always out front beating a clear path through time. When the father is gone so is the guidance. The son must now face the uncertain future on his own and is always in danger of getting off the path.

My mother seldom talked about him after his funeral. She realized she had to get on with her own life. We did go to the cemetery to visit both Edward's and his grave quite regularly. Within a few years, however, my mother met and married her second husband and moved forward as best she could. I did not call my replacement father "Tata." To me, Alex was always "Pa."

The Polish property mentioned above was bought or somehow acquired near the end of the Depression. It may even have been accepted as payment for one of the foreclosed mortgages that he held. In any case, the property was conveniently located near the village where he was born and was tilled and worked by members of his own family.

I suspect he intended to return to his former homeland and resume being a simple farmer. Unfortunately for him (but fortunately for me) world affairs in the form of wars and years of Soviet subjugation voided this plan.

Ownership of this land passed on to me, the sole male heir, after his death. (For a short time I was one of the landed gentry — a veritable Polish Prince!)

In the late 60s when my mother visited Poland, she took with her an official-looking Polish document that I had signed with which I deeded the land to one of my cousins who had been working the land for years. I have no idea where this property is located or the name of its current owner.

PERSPECTIVE: I often wonder how different my life would have been if Tata had not died. I'm absolutely certain that my relationship with my mother would have been much less adversarial. In addition, with his support (and possibly, greater wisdom) the family may not have ended up in a run-down neighborhood. This change alone would have made a major difference in my view of life.

I can't say that I missed him after he died because, honestly, I really didn't know him. However, I somehow miss him now.

6

Friends

I always hung around with kids younger than myself for several reasons, the most obvious of which was that I was very immature. I just could not keep up with members of my peer group from school. They all seemed wiser and totally 'with it' whereas I just didn't get it, no matter what 'it' was. Consequently, kids who were a year or two younger were about right for my social and mental age.

Billy was one of my closest friends. He was about a year younger than I and the second oldest of four brothers. The family lived at the end of our block above the corner tavern which was owned and operated by his parents.

The parents also came from Poland and chose to earn a living by serving beer and lunch sandwiches to the many factory workers who labored nearby. Their establishment was far from fancy because the family was even poorer than most others on the block. Because of this tough background, he was, at a very early age, like Fagin, one of those desperately-clever kid characters out of *Oliver Twist*.

Incidentally, we both had the distinction of being the only kids on the block who were known by our foreign names. I was called Jasiu, and he went by the Polish equivalent of Billy, or "Bolek."

The four boys in his family shared a common feature that made them easy to describe and identify — they all had green teeth! Now I must admit that I didn't brush my teeth very often, but certainly I did it more often than never. Because of their poor oral hygienic habits, they lost their teeth early. Bolek's older brother had a few gaps in his mouth before he entered his teens. Their overall personal hygiene also suffered because they did not have a bathtub in the house. On the rare occasion when they did bathe, they did so in the center of the kitchen using a galvanized washtub.

In spite of all these handicaps, Billy had a good attitude about life. He also knew that if he was going to succeed in any way, it would have to be through his own efforts and pluck: no one was going to give him anything except, maybe grief.

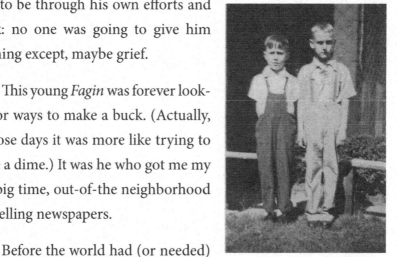

This young *Fagin* was forever looking for ways to make a buck. (Actually, in those days it was more like trying to make a dime.) It was he who got me my first big time, out-of-the neighborhood job, selling newspapers.

Before the world had (or needed) instant news, every busy street corner in the city had at least one newsstand that was operated by a kid or by an older, semi-street-person. My first job was tending the least busy of three newspaper stands on the corner of California and North Avenues located about three miles from my house. This was a busy corner where two streetcar lines crossed and there was a lot of foot traffic as people changed from one line to the other.

Immediately after school, Bolek and I would hop on the Division Street streetcar then transfer to the California line so we could get to our assigned newsstands in time to set up and serve the coming-home crowd during the afternoon rush-hour. I was eleven years old.

Bolek showed me the ropes. He taught me how to make change from a little two-pocket apron and then later from one of those really neat, belt-mounted, thumb-operated change machines. I also learned how to really "sell" papers. We didn't just stand there waiting for customers. We yelled out headlines both real and imaginary, accosted people as they walked by and, generally, acted like newsboys did in the B-movies of the time.

"EXTRA, EXTRA, read all about it."

In those days Chicago had five major daily newspapers and we were given a different quota of each to sell. Because we didn't want to have any papers left over at the end of the day, we had to push the less popular papers along with the ones that had a loyal following and sold themselves. What made it even more challenging was that several editions of each newspaper often came out during the day, and even an occasional red-inked EXTRA had to be presented (or hawked) to all passersby in hopes of selling even more papers.

Our job was made somewhat simpler by the fact that there was no TV news to watch when the commuters got home. I did learn, however, that it wasn't easy to convince people that the paper they may have bought earlier in the day had really old news in it and that they should buy another one from us which had new news. All of this so they could take it home and "read all about it." The whole concept was very eye opening. It was a real job and I was part of the real world.

Among other tricks-of-the-trade, Bolek showed me how to hold a stack of papers under my arm, newest edition on the top, older ones behind, and how to deal off of the bottom of the stack. This was a good way for us to unload older papers on unsuspecting customers who did not stop to examine what they had just purchased.

He used this bait-and-switch technique very effectively and often managed to unload leftover papers from the previous day, thereby realizing a total profit on the transaction. The ever-present risk of being caught and possibly attacked by an irate customer seemed to me to not be worth the scam.

He also tried to teach me how to short-change customers. In spite of my efforts, I found this trick very hard to do because of the money levels we dealt with. When a paper costs five cents and the customer gives you a dime, there isn't much maneuvering room to do much cheating. Bolek somehow managed to do it more often than most. (Four cents change instead of a nickel yielded a pirated profit of one cent. Wow! Not worth the risk.)

After working the corner stands for a while, Bolek and I got a chance to move up in the brotherhood of newspaper vendors to a different level of selling: we became 'hustlers.'

We no longer had a fixed location where we sold the papers from a newsstand. We were driven out to our territory by the newspaper distributor and given a stack of papers which we sold while on the move. The downside of this assignment was that we worked nights — from about 6 pm until almost midnight.

After an evening of hustling, we were again picked up by the distributor and driven home. This last portion made it a bit better than taking a late-night streetcar, but not too by much.

My first assignment was in the nightclub district located way out in the suburbs at the corner of North and Harlem Avenues. (The city has since expanded so this area is now considered to be in-town.) My job was to go from restaurant to restaurant, walk among the tables, and try to sell papers to the customers.

It must have been annoying to some of the well-dressed patrons to be bothered by us little, poorly-dressed wretches. For some reason though, the management did allow us to come inside, and we did sell a lot of papers. Most of the purchases, I'm sure, were made because of pity, or in an attempt to impress the girlfriend by giving the smelly kid a big tip. Either way, it was okay by me.

I was soon befriended/pitied by one of the cooks at a small restaurant. He regularly bought a paper which he probably didn't need or read and would occasionally feed me.

The restaurant's specialty was pork barbecue sandwiches served with coleslaw and fries. I was allowed to eat this wonderful foreign food in his warm kitchen off a paper plate while he read the paper and pretended to discuss world events with me. Such elegant and exotic dining was simply not available to me at home.

Since all the restaurants were not conveniently located close together, I had to walk from one group to the next over a distance of several blocks. Because every place was out in the boonies, I had to walk along the dark roads without benefit of sidewalks or street lighting. If the weather was wet or cold, I would often hitchhike from one area to the next.

Today it's hard to imagine surviving in that type of environment where our innocence was our only shield.

Luckily for us, most people driving by would stop if they saw a newsboy with his thumb out. If the driver had his wife with him, I could usually see she would be visibly disturbed that a kid my size was out alone at night hitching a ride. She would want to know how old I was and why I was out on the street at this late hour and other motherly things. I quickly learned to mumble a memorized, suitably-sad answer which almost always guaranteed that a paper would be sold before we got to the end of the ride.

Thank you again, Bolek.

Billy had a lot of gimmicks, and he especially knew how to work a Christmas crowd. His best trick was to tie a piece of mistletoe to the end of a stick and then hold it over the head of a customer's girlfriend. The guy got an unexpected kiss and Bolek sold a paper, usually with a nice tip attached.

Of the ten or so nightclubs I visited on a nightly basis, I remember one that was especially elegant (to my untrained eyes, anyway).

It was called "The Homestead." It always seemed to have the nicest crowds and the waiters were very well appointed.

I made my rounds there several times each evening and this is where I got by largest tip. It happened during the Christmas season. Snow was falling and I came in with just enough of it on my shoulders and knitted Navy-surplus cap to look authentically pitiful. I approached a huge corner table that held what seemed to be a family gathering of about ten or more adults and children. Some of the kids were about my age.

At the head of the table was an elegant gentleman who seemed to be in charge of the group, so I went up to him first. He not only bought a paper but also ordered one for everyone seated at the table.

Cool!

When he asked me the total price, I gave the correct answer without hesitation. He pretended to be very impressed with my ability to multiply by five and announced to all seated that I would someday be a successful businessman, possibly like himself. (He was wrong.) He then gave me a five-dollar bill and told me to keep the change! Very impressive! I wished them all a Merry Christmas as I went out into the night, resolved to someday to return to this fine establishment not as an urchin, but as a respectable paying guest.[9]

I can now imagine the scene that transpired after I left the room: the kids seated at the table were given a lecture by their parents on how fortunate they were and then I was used as a wretched

---

9 I did return years later only to find the place no longer existed and had been demolished after a partial fire. It was rumored that the Mafia was somehow involved. Could be.

example of what could happen to them if they did not apply themselves. (I wonder if it did any of them a bit of good.) Meanwhile, I was very happy to have sold my night's quota of papers so early in the evening.

During the summer months when the trotters (sulky race horses) were running, we hustlers would work at several racetracks. The track was a good place to work because it closed earlier than the nightclubs and there were many more potential customers.

Some of these customers were drunk, others were big winners, but the best customers were drunken, big winners. They were almost guaranteed to tip a buck or two and sometimes not even take a paper.

I soon got tired of the hustling circuit and let Bolek educate my eager replacement. Coming home around midnight every night was a bit too much. In addition, my grades suffered as a result, and something had to be done.

It was then that I applied for and got a respectable newspaper job — home delivery.

It was close to home and was my first day job. As luck would have it, I landed an easy route assignment. It was four blocks long beginning at the distributor's office and ending near my house. Perfect! It only took about 30 minutes tops to run every day after school plus Saturday and Sunday mornings.

We delivered the papers while riding our bikes. We carried the papers in a large canvas bag slung either over the handlebars or over one shoulder. In either mode, balancing the load while peddling, steering and throwing papers was quite an accomplishment.

On Sundays when the papers were twice as heavy, we either left the distributor's office with two bags full or with half a load, which required coming back for the second half mid-way through the route. Either way, Sundays were much harder. Several times when my bike developed an overnight flat I had to deliver my route on foot or by pulling a wagonload of papers.

We also had to resort to wagon pulling following a deep snowfall. And worse yet, when the weather got really bad, it was down to sleds. In any case, paper delivery was easier than working the nightclub circuit. The really hard part of the job was collecting weekly fees for our services.

Every week we had to knock on each customer's door and collect the paltry sum of 40 cents. It still amazes me how few tips we got and how many people would purposefully try to stiff us. They all took advantage of the delivery boy because they knew he would carry them for a few weeks without being paid. Then, when they finally answered our knock at the door, they could not believe that it had been that long ago since they last paid. Well, it was, and guess who was paying for your daily paper for all those weeks?

As I stated above, the job did not bring in many tips, especially not for me. As usual, my problem was in my delivery. All of us paper boys had this special way of rolling the newspaper — without the use of rubber bands or plastic bags — so that it could be thrown onto the porch from the street or sidewalk.

Many guys suffered from lack of accuracy and hit the bushes instead of the porch. That was not my problem. I could hit the center of every porch. My problem was the way I rolled the paper. I swear I did it exactly the same way as everyone else. In my case, however, the paper would open up in flight about three feet above the porch. (My exclusive parachute roll!)

I remember a few times returning to the distributor's office after completing my route only to see several of my customers retrieving their papers one page at a time after the wind got hold of them. Needless to say, after a few well-founded customer complaints, the distributor requested I "go on vacation for a while." I believe I'm still officially on vacation from that job.

So there I was, almost 12 years old and without a job.

As luck would have it, the delivery boy at the grocery store my mother visited most often was quitting. When she found out about it she sent me there to immediately apply for the job. I guess even then I took good job interviews because I got hired.

It was a terrific job. I only had to work on Saturday afternoons during the school year and six days a week during the summer months. I was paid ten cents an hour plus tips.

The grocery store was like any one of a dozen other family-run neighborhood businesses. Very small, no variety, and high prices. Its main distinguishing feature was that the owner (Chester) spoke Polish to his customers and that's what they wanted to hear.

His wife Marge did not speak Polish. She was a fairly attractive, modern woman which made her the constant target of verbal abuse by the non-attractive, old-fashioned customers. They felt free to say nasty things about her in Polish, even in her presence. This practice soon stopped when they found out I not only understood their remarks, but would relay them to Marge after they left.

Chester's now-frail and sickly father originally started the business. He lived with Chester's family and helped wherever he could. His duties were mainly confined to the basement where he prepared (another word for killed) chickens. My duties included stocking shelves, sweeping floors, delivering groceries and helping grandpa in the basement.

A small flock of live chickens was tended by grandpa and kept in a coop out in back of the store. If a customer wanted a chicken, Chester would run out to the coop, pick out one or two and bring them in for the customer to choose.

After a selection was made, I would carry the victim downstairs where grandpa would dispatch it with a hatchet and throw it into a bloody barrel where it thrashed around for a while. When the spasms ceased, grandpa would dunk it in a cauldron of boiling water and remove all of its feathers. The bird would then be cut open and the innards removed. All of the requested parts were then wrapped in butcher paper and taken upstairs for the customer who was completing her shopping.

It was an amazingly efficient (albeit primitive and bloody) operation. From coop to hatchet to wrapping paper didn't take longer than 15 minutes. I often helped with the evisceration when there were many birds being processed. I bet I could still peel a gizzard without spilling the bile sack. (Small explanation: the gizzard or stomach contains undigested grain that must be removed before the customer can cook it. The bile sack is a small organ next to the stomach, which must be carefully removed because it contains a bitter liquid that will ruin the taste of the meat if it is punctured.)

Of all of my tasks, grocery delivery was the most important. Almost all our customers were people from the immediate neighborhood. Everyone walked to the store, no one drove. Some of the ladies were quite old and could not carry the groceries home with them, even if it was only a short walk. This is where I came in: to provide the free home delivery. (Chester Inc. provided free home delivery long before there was an Amazon Inc.)

I would pack the groceries into a cardboard box and load it onto my wagon. I would then walk with the customer to her house and carry the groceries into the kitchen. As we walked, I would talk to the lady in Polish to endear myself thereby hoping to increase my tip. (Thank you again, Bolek).

Most of these women were friends of my mother so I had to be on my best behavior at all times or a report would be sent home on the PMN (Polish Mother's Network). Depending on the size of the load, and the level or schmoozing, I would get a dime, or sometimes as much as a quarter for my efforts.

I remember one of our customers who lived about two blocks from the store. She was a "Blue Star Mother" and very proud of it. All five of her sons served in the WWII simultaneously. She kept the distinctive white flag with its five blue stars arranged in a circle hanging in the front window long after the war ended and all five sons returned home safely. She also made huge grocery purchases to feed these guys and was always good for a quarter tip whenever I made a delivery.

Some customers were true shut-ins and could not come to the store. They would phone-in their orders and I would fill them. Then, since these orders were usually small, I would deliver the purchased groceries to their homes on my bike.

If the customer did not have an account at the store and could not buy on credit, I had to collect. C.O.D. as it were. Marge would give me change for a five- or ten-dollar bill to make it easy on the customer.

These orders, which required the most effort, should have produced the largest tips, but they did not because they came from the poorest of our clientele.

In addition to stocking shelves, helping grandpa with the chickens and delivering groceries, I would often accompany Chester on store-restocking trips. This meant an early-morning trip in his giant station wagon to the huge IGA (Independent Grocers Alliance) warehouse located near downtown.

At the time there were very few supermarkets in the city. Most neighborhood grocery stores were of the Mom-n-Pop variety, and almost all of them were members of the IGA. Since they were small operations, they had no leverage with the giant food suppliers. Being part of this co-op allowed them to buy many different food products at one location and at a slightly lower price.

At the warehouse I would push/pull a low-boy cart through the aisles while Chester loaded it with items he knew his customers were sure to buy. (Every trip I make to COSTCO reminds me of this part of my retail experience.)

The really neat part of this "adventure" was when we would don huge fur-lined coats before entering the meat-freezer section of the warehouse. Chester would then select one or more huge hunks of beef/pork and add them to our cart.

Selecting the meat was the most critical portion of the trip. Not only was this the single most expensive item on his shopping list, but he also had to be absolutely certain that it was exactly what his customers would want to buy during the following week.

I don't remember telling any of my schoolmates about my experiences in the grocery business. The fact that I had a regular paying job made me different enough.

I usually gave all the money I earned to my mother, but sometimes I held back a little. Over the years I had amassed enough to buy a stolen pellet pistol. (I bought it from my local candy store operator who did a little hot-merchandise fencing on the side.)

All the guys had BB-guns, and that was no big deal, but a pellet pistol, now that was heavy armament. I knew that even my mother would recognize this as a weapon of mass destruction and not a toy suitable for a kid, so I hid it inside the piano. Every once in a while I would get it out of its hiding place and accidentally put a hole through something.

After working in the grocery business for a couple of years, I had to quit because it was time to go off to high school.

I did go back and visit with Marge and Chester when I was home on vacation, but these visits did not last long, and neither did the store. An A&P supermarket opened up a few blocks away and Chester just could not compete.

PERSPECTIVE: Yes, I lived a tough life, but so did the rest of the kids in the neighborhood. The tough part was also the normal part.

7

Bob

I do not remember when Bob and I got to be friends. Probably shortly after we moved to Crystal Street. My mother did not want me to hang around with him because he wasn't a Catholic. (Like that made a difference to a kid.)

His family lived at the end of the block on the top floor of a three-flat. Bob's family was unusual in several respects, many of which should have made us totally incompatible. First of all, there was that Catholic thing, (2) they were not Polish, (3) they were tenants not owners; and, worst yet, (4) Bob went to public school. In spite of all these otherwise damning social differences, Bob and I remained friends for a long time because we shared in a unifying weirdness — we were both firebugs.

If there was anything happening that involved fire or an explosion, we were there. Sometimes only as innocent observers, other times as the causes of the excitement. Almost all of my memories of Bob involve some form of blaze or blast, and not always an intentional one.

Once we were out on a bike ride and took a short cut through the back property of a nearby foundry. The property was quite huge and contained some abandoned buildings, one of which we decided to explore.

I have no idea what the original purpose of the building was, but it was a large structure built of massive wooden beams. I suspect it may have been a sawmill at one time. In any case, the floors were strewn with trash and paper and there was not much to see or swipe.

Just before we left, Bob found a huge fuse box mounted on a wall and decided that he wanted to break the porcelain fuse-holders inside, so he began beating on them with a piece of pipe. He wasn't making satisfactory progress (hard to define in this case) when I looked outside and told him to stop. I had noticed some power lines were still connected to the building and, possibly, to the very fuse box he was trying to destroy.

Bob decided to stop and get on with our trip home.

After we had gone about a mile, we were passed by several fire engines going in the opposite direction. Since that could only mean fire — our middle names — we turned around and followed the trucks. It soon became obvious where they were going and why.

The entire structure we had just explored was engulfed in flames and could not be extinguished. In fact the firemen really didn't do much to save it since it did not endanger any other property, and so it burned to the ground. Even though a fire scene of this magnitude would normally have held us both spellbound for hours, we were smart enough not to hang around when the Fire Investigators got there.

The other big fire episode involving both of us occurred right after Christmas. In years past the neighborhood guys would gather tossed-out Christmas trees in the empty lot on the corner and then, after we had collected enough of them, we'd set them on fire. The blaze usually got quite large and some neighbor would, for some unknown reason, summon the fire department to put an end to the fun.

But that year we planned ahead. Instead of alerting the neighbors of our intentions by stockpiling the dead trees in the lot, we hid small collections of them in several locations. Then, at a pre-set time, we quickly gathered them together and set a massive bonfire before the authorities could be notified. It was a fabulous blaze that was talked about for the remainder of the winter.

Of all the moronic things we did (and there were many), episodes of airplane burning were the dumbest. Like most boys at the time, Bob and I liked to build model airplanes. The big difference with our efforts was that we didn't fly them or display them. These planes were built with only one objective in mind — to be burned.

These were large wingspan, balsa stick-and-tissue paper models that took a long time (and some talent) to build. Hundreds of pieces had to be cut, shaped, assembled, a paper-covering applied, and a rubber-band motor installed.

After weeks of dedicated labor, the finished model would be flight-tested a few times to determine its airborne characteristics. Then, after every surface was trimmed and adjusted just right, we would go up to Bob's back porch and, from the vantage of the third floor, set the plane on fire as we launched it toward the alley.

Sometimes the stricken plane would glide all the way to the alley, then crash and burn. Other times it would collapse in-flight and fall in a mass of blazing balsa struts. I'm still not too certain which scenario was better. However, in all cases, the total on-fire flight time would be less than ten seconds. All of the flights were good, I think, and each was well worth the effort.

Sometimes, just for variety's sake, we would load a few firecrackers on the plane as cargo. Although the effect was more dramatic, it was not nearly as dependable as a good-old, in-air fire. Besides, explosives had other uses.

Fireworks were really easy to come by at the time. Some comic books even featured ads from mail-order distributors. All one had to do was send some money to this one company in Ohio and they would gladly send a huge box of all kind of goodies by return mail. What could be easier than that? The strange thing about it was that no proof of age or maturity required — neither of which we had in any abundance.

These fireworks assortments included many different types and sizes of firecrackers plus rockets, cones and pinwheels. Upon receipt of the package, we would lay them all out in some logical order of mayhem.

My favorite brand of firecracker was called the Red White and Blue. These came tied together in a cylindrical shape, 100 crackers to a package. The best part was all the wicks were not braided together as was the case with other popular brands such as the Zebra brand. The RWBs could easily be set off one at a time without having to unravel each wick.

Of course, the best weapon of all was the M-80. These were more like little bombs then crackers. They were squat little silver cylinders, each with its wick coming out of the side instead of the end. Also, the wicks were waterproof so they could be weighted with a rock and dropped into a pond or deep puddle. This feature made depth-charging of frogs not only possible but also very easy.

The most menacing of all were the Cherry Bombs. This is a very descriptive name for these bright-red, plum-sized lumps of dynamite. They were rare because of their high price and were usually reserved for situations that called for mass destruction.

There were times when we needed to light a series of firecrackers quickly, one after another, and that is when individual match-lighting was just far too slow.[10] This is where 'punks' came in handy. Every summer we would bike over to a small swamp located near the railroad tracks and harvest a huge supply of cattails. These would then be set out to dry in the sunlight on a garage or shed roof. When the stems were no longer green, they would be stored away for future use.[11]

Fireworks were used to blow up all sorts of things: tin cans, small tunnels dug in the dirt, toy soldiers and, of course, bottles (dumb!). But, the most fun was making grenades.

There was a huge apple tree on the block that produced inedible green apples around the 4th of July. We would use a stick or a nail to

10 No one ever set off a full string of firecrackers all at once. That was far too wasteful. They were always unraveled and lit individually to make the mystical experience last longer.

11 Dried cattails or punks were used as follows: the end was snipped off and lit with a match. Since the lit end would burn very slowly (smolder really), it could be used to light the wick of any firework.

poke a hole in an apple, insert and light a firecracker, and then throw it at a similarly-armed band of lunatics located across the street.

The object, of course, was to hold the apple-grenade while the wick burned down far enough so that it would explode in-flight above the heads of our enemy. If you held it too long, no big deal. All you got was a handful of applesauce. (Could it be that too many grenades went off close to my ears so that now I have to wear hearing aids?)

I usually didn't keep or use all the fireworks I bought. I learned early on that it was much smarter to buy them in large quantities (wholesale?) and sell them piecemeal (retail?) for an enormous profit. The money realized could then be used to buy more supplies. Was I a decadent young capitalist, or what?

Bob's greatest explosive "achievement" happened just before we graduated from grade school, and I was not with him at the time. (Honest, I have an alibi.) He told the story of how he tried to throw a lit cracker through an air vent on the roof of a nearby furniture factory. (Don't ask why.)

After many unsuccessful attempts, he was about to give up when one got through. It fell inside, exploded, and the blast ignited a sawdust-explosion that blew out the windows and burned the place down. Who said fireworks were dangerous?

Although I later saw the burned-out building that was allegedly claimed by Bob's firecracker, I started to doubt many of his other stories. As kids, we all stretched the truth about almost everything. That was a fact. However, it seems he started to exaggerate a little too much about his exploits, what his relatives did, or what he saw someplace else. Worst yet, I think he started to believe some of his own stories.

It soon became clear to me that Bob was just a big liar and I could not trust him anymore. This was a terrible thing to learn for a kid and, likewise, even harder to resolve.

Bob and I soon drifted apart. When the trust was gone, we had little in common. I went off to an out-of-town high school while he stayed in Chicago and attended public high where he did not do well scholastically. I remember we met just before I enrolled at IIT.[12] Sure we'd meet and talk once in a while but I could see we were on vastly different paths, ones that would probably never cross again.

PERSPECTIVE: Learning about human nature first-hand is a real downer.

---

12 Illinois Institute of Technology.

8

Streetcars

Two types of streetcars were in use in Chicago when I was a kid. These were the sleek, newer "Green Hornets" which served the downtown area and the old "Red Rockets" that took care of the out-lying areas. (Those probably were not their official names, but that was what we called them.) Both types ran on tracks down the center of the street. The rails were not like an exposed railroad track but were flat grooved, steel ribbons set flush into a wide strip of cobble-stones. The car wheels ran on the flat part of the track and the wheel's flange was set in the groove to keep it from wandering off.

I bring up these details because we often would place pennies (or stones or other experimental objects) on the flat part of the track so that the car would run over them and flatten them out. The prob-lem was to recover the flattened object after its violent encounter because the car's weight would often pressure-weld it to the wheel or to the track.

A story that made the rounds (probably apocryphal) related to how some kids greased the track at the bottom of a slight hill and as the streetcar came down the hill, it failed to stop and skidded through an intersection causing an accident. This tale probably was not true because there are no hills of any consequence in Chicago. But it was a good story. One we loved to think about. I'm quite certain if we could somehow find a lot of grease (and a hill), we would have tried it ourselves.

Red Rockets were, first of all, red and very boxy. They were designed symmetrically about the middle and could go in either direction. The motorman was in front and the conductor was stationed in the rear. Electrical power to run the car was received through a spring-loaded trolley located in the rear, and it pushed upwards against an overhead wire. The cars had two trolley assemblies, one at each end. Whichever one was connected determined which direction the car would go. Both trolleys were operated with attached ropes and the unused front trolley was secured by a large hook on the roof.

Really mischievous kids would often reach out the open rear window and pull the trolley rope and disconnect the car from the overhead wire and bringing it to a halt. The conductor would then have to get out and reconnect the trolley — which took some skill and usually produced a large shower of sparks as the connection was briefly made and then lost.

Green Hornet cars were more modern. Because they had a defined front and rear they had to loop around a block at the end of a line to turn around. We seldom rode these cars. They mostly operated downtown which, though only eight miles away, was considered to be a foreign country and was seldom visited.

The Red Rockets had many unique features, one of which was the passenger seat backs which were mounted on pivots. This was done so each seat could be reversed at the end of the line and face in the other direction. One advantage of the pivoting seat back was if a group of four friends was riding together, they could flip a seat back to form a face-to-face seating/conversation arrangement (_ _/).

Another strange feature was that each car carried a goodly supply of sand. This was stored at both ends of the car just above the track and in front of the wheels. In winter when the tracks were frozen, braking friction was very poor. When the motorman felt the car could slide beyond a stop he would pull a lever and dump some sand onto the track to help stop the car. It may have been very primitive but it also was very effective.

Because the cars were often full to capacity during rush hours, there were not enough seats for all passengers and some had to stand in the aisle. Their ride would have been extremely uncomfortable had it not been for several "steadying" features. These consisted of floor-to-ceiling shiny chrome poles located along the length of the central aisle for standing passengers to hold and keep themselves from toppling over when subjected to the car's often erratic movements.

Another balancing aid was a series of leather straps that hung down from a horizontal bar located near the ceiling. Each strap ended in a leather loop, the bottom of which was about six feet above the floor. In addition to their designed purpose of steadying passengers, they also served a second, unplanned-for purpose: they provided a test for an unofficial rite of passage from kidhood. When you finally were tall enough to grab onto the strap's loop, you knew you were no longer a little kid but had moved one step closer to being a real adult.

Because the cars ran on tracks located near the center of the street, passengers had to board and exit right in the middle of traffic. (Fortunately, auto traffic was very light so the number of accidents was kept relatively low.) In order to further protect the waiting passengers from being run down, the city built loading zones or "safety islands" at every major stop. Each island was about 30 feet long, four-to-six feet wide, and six inches above the street. It also had a huge protective concrete nose at one end facing into the flow of traffic. These formidable structures were not really needed out in the outskirts of the city where there was little auto traffic, but were absolutely necessary throughout the downtown area.

The theory of a safety island was that passengers would safely wait on the curb until a streetcar was in sight. They would then move out to the island for boarding. Unfortunately this convention did not always work. When there were many people waiting, the same orderly queue could not be established on the curb and then maintained out on the island. Consequently, people tended not wait at the curb for the streetcar but stood on the island. This created quite a sight. Forty or more people crowded onto a narrow concrete "raft" anchored in a river of traffic flowing by just inches away. A slight jostle and someone was in the street.

Island, yes — Safety Island, no.

When the streetcar would finally arrive, riders got on at the rear, paid the conductor and moved forward into the passenger compartment. One could exit from either end, but front exiting was encouraged. The conductor collected fares, issued transfers and also collected transfers. He was very busy during rush hour, so it was easy to ride a short distance without paying by simply not moving off the entry platform. Transfers were issued on-request and were needed when making a connection onto an intersecting line.

One money-saving trick some people used only worked during busy rush hours. The object was to sneak onto the streetcar without paying, wait a little while, and then go back to the conductor and tell him that you forgot to get a transfer when you paid your fare. If the story worked, not only was the price of the fare saved, but the transfer to the next streetcar would be hassle-free.

Most passengers got into the habit of asking for a transfer whether they needed it or not. Then, if they did not need it, they simply threw it away. It was not unusual to see dozens of transfers fluttering in a strong Chicago wind or otherwise littering any avenue equipped with a streetcar line.

On hot summer afternoons my friends and I would often take a ride on the streetcar to cool off. At the half-fare price of only four cents, it was worth it. We had a good time riding along with the windows open and a breeze blowing through the semi-empty car. We would go to the end of the line, not get off, and then just ride back to our starting point.

I always was fascinated by the motorman's job and liked to watch him perform his duties while I stood next to him and looked out the front window as we careened down Division Street. The truth is, operating a streetcar was a tough job.

Neither the motorman nor the conductor had seats and had to stand the full time. The conductor could, of course, occasionally sit in an unused passenger seat, but I'm sure this practice was frowned upon by management. The best the motorman could do was lean back against a metal fence located just behind him.

This fence was made out of bent pipe and was the shape of a huge staple. It was set into two holes in the floor and it, too, had to be moved to the other end of the car when reversing its direction. Note that the fence was not there for the motorman's comfort, but served as a barrier to keep the passengers from pressing in on him and interfering with the car's operation under crowded conditions.

About once a year a few classes from our grade school would go on a field trip. Since there were no school buses available to transport the 20 or 30 students involved, the school would charter a streetcar for the journey. We each had to pay something extra for this excursion, but I'm sure it wasn't very much, probably only a quarter.

All the students going on the trip would be marched about a block to the nearest streetcar stop located on the corner of Kostner and Chicago Avenues. There, at a pre-arranged time, our chartered streetcar would arrive. We would board and proceed to our destination. One popular place was the Field Museum located on the Michigan lakefront. Since the tracks on Chicago Avenue did not go directly to the museum, the car had to be switched onto other lines and work its way diagonally across the city.

This was quite an involved procedure. The conductor would get out at an intersection carrying a long-handled tool. He would insert it into a hole in the street and, by turning the crank several times, the track would be switched. The car would then move forward a little (blocking traffic all the while) and wait while the Conductor restored the switch points to their normal positions before re-boarding.

This ritual had to be performed many times along the way until we finally zigzagged from the North Side of Chicago to the South Side. The entire track-switching process then had to be reversed on our return trip.

One horrible accident involving a streetcar occurred in the late 1940s when a crowded Green Hornet smashed into the side of a tanker truck carrying gasoline. The fuel spilled onto the street and burst into flame incinerating all on board. No one could get out because all windows had bars on them and the doors (which opened inwardly) were jammed shut by the press of the crowd. The city's response to the accident was to bar gasoline trucks from traveling on that particular street.

Some solution!

By the end of the 50s all of Chicago's streetcars were gone. The tracks were either torn up or covered, and all the routes were taken over by either diesel or trolley buses. It truly was the end of an era. Too bad. No longer was it possible for a kid to stand up front next to the motorman, look out the front window and pretend to be driving a Red Rocket as it careened down the center of Division Street.

PERSPECTIVE: Strange how the trolley cycle repeats itself. Now that all the rails have been torn up, plans are being made to bring them back.

9

Games

I don't remember playing any games or having any specific toys before moving to Crystal Street. There were many kids of all ages in that neighborhood and we interacted on a daily basis. Gamesmanship and strategies were taught in an apprentice-like manner. Older kids played semi-organized games of softball and football and numerous card and marble games. Little kids were allowed to watch the big kids play until they learned the rules and strategies. Once they were deemed ready they were brought into the game as full-fledged members.

Softball (we called it baseball because we didn't know any better) was played in several places: on the street, in an empty lot, or even in the alley.

Chicago-style softball is played differently than almost anywhere else. The main difference is the ball is huge — sixteen inches in circumference instead of the more familiar twelve inches. Because of its large size and weight, the ball could not be hit very far making it perfect for playing in a confined area. Because a 40-foot blast would probably be stretched into a home run, the outfielders stood just beyond the edge of the base paths, and acted as back-ups to the infielders who got most of the fielding action.

Another reason none of the hits went very far was because the one ball we had was so old and well-used it resembled — and behaved like — a spherical pillow. Consequently, there was no "crack of the bat." It was more of a "thud" or even a "swoosh" as air was expelled from the loose outer covering. And it's a good thing the ball was soft because we didn't need to use gloves. Besides, we certainly couldn't afford to buy them anyway.

We seldom could field enough players for two teams so we played "move up." Two or three players were on the batting team and everyone else was on the field. Each batter stayed on the batting team until he made an out. He then moved to the furthest-most field position, and all other fielders moved up one position. (Hence the name of the game.)

Typically, the last field position was right-fielder and the position just prior to joining the batting team was pitcher. Sometimes, when we were really short-handed, we played without a right-fielder and any ball hit to that field was ruled an out. We had to learn early how to place the ball or else we spent very little time on the batting team. The big advantage of the move up scheme is that it exposed us to all of the positions on the field. There was no room for specialization when we always were a few players short.

Stickball — the big city version of baseball — was also played. The rules were the same as softball/baseball except that we used a cut-off broom handle as the bat and a tennis ball instead of a baseball.

Pitching was overhand and we didn't need a catcher because we played up against a brick wall which bounced the ball back to the pitcher. A one-size-fits-all strike zone was drawn on the wall behind the batter.

Football was played for only a short interval of time before snow depths prevented any outside play. Basketball and soccer were unknown in our neighborhood. I know both had been invented a long time back, but I did not experience either one before entering high school.

Some activities had seasons associated with them. Each of these seasons was quite short — just a few weeks during which time everyone did only one thing: flew a kite, spun a top, flipped a yo-yo, or maybe roller-skated. I don't know who was in charge of this, but each season of feverish activity began and ended rather abruptly.

A season could be in full swing and all of the kids would finally be getting good at whatever the activity was, and bang, that season would end and be replaced by another. It did not matter that you were a good top-spinner but a rotten yo-yoer. When the top-spinning season ended, you dropped your spiker and picked up the Duncan because it was not fashionable to be caught participating in the wrong activity after its season had been declared officially over.

Many games were played on the narrow patch of dirt between the curb and the sidewalk; others were played on the street. Since there were so few cars, the side streets were almost always empty with maybe one or two parked cars per block. (Passing traffic amounted to, at most, one car per hour.)

With the onset of TV and video games, almost all street activities ended. It is quite possible today that none of the games we played are being played anywhere.

Note that the rules and description of several other popular games appear in an addendum. Considering the low quality of today's TV game shows, maybe some of these games could be adopted for TV programming, but that's highly unlikely.

The following are rules to only two "games" which, in themselves are so weird; they demand to be immediately mentioned.

The wildest, weirdest and most violent of the off-street games was Buck-Buck. It required a relatively large number of participants to do it "right" and therefore was seldom played. It also seldom ended amicably or without injury which made it even more interesting.

Rules for Buck-Buck

Two teams of four to six players each were selected. One of the teams was designated as the first victim by whatever means. One player — usually the or lamp pole. The next member did the same, but instead of grabbing the pole, he held onto the waist of the first guy. This bend-and-grab sequence continued until a chain of human backs was formed. (Not the kind of game one would want to play after a lunch of rice and beans.)

Now, here comes the really weird part, one that any psychiatrist would have a field day analyzing: all of the members of the opposite team would jump onto this platform of backs, one at a time in a leap-frog manner. When they were all off the ground and clutching on to each other, the on-top team captain held up zero to five fingers and asked the underneath captain "Buck-buck, how many fingers up?"

If he guessed correctly, they changed sides. If he failed on three guesses, they didn't change sides and the top team did another leap. Also, if the lower team collapsed from the weight, they had to repeat the setup. However, if anyone on the on-top team fell off, then the sides switched. Weird!

The whole guessing process of how many fingers were showing was based upon honesty since no one in the lower team could see the fingers and thereby verify the number. But it all worked out somehow since kids are basically honest at that age.

Rules for Knuckles

The game was played with a regular deck of cards with rules similar to Crazy-8, except there were no wild cards, and there was a different pay-off at the end. Five cards were dealt to each player, and the top card of the deck turned over. The remaining cards were placed face-down in a pile. Each player would take a turn placing a card from his hand on the face-up stack. The card played could either be in-suit or matching the top card, thereby changing the suit. If not able to play a card, the player would draw from the deck (dig) until a match was found. The object was to get rid of all cards in the hand. Play continued until only one player had cards in his hand. He was the victim.

After the loser had been identified, he then made a tight fist and extended his hand. Each of the other players took a turn hitting him on his knuckles with the full deck of cards. The number of hits corresponded to the number of cards remaining in his hand at the end of the game.

Hits were administered in a vicious, downward, scraping fashion using the exposed edge of the deck. The sole purpose, of course, was to break the skin on the knuckles and draw some blood. (Charming!)

Several rules of protocol were also enforced, the most important of which was: if the victim flinched (pulled back), the number of hits was doubled. (More charming!)

A very strict set of rules also applied to those administering the hits. Each hitter was only allowed to hold the deck with one hand after the hitting sequence began. If the hitter touched the deck with both hands before administering all the required whacks, he received the full number of hits from the former victim. In addition, if the hitter accidentally dropped the card deck before completing his executioner duties, he received 52 hits from the ex-victim. (We quickly learned how to hold onto the deck at all costs.)

At times there wasn't a kid on the block who didn't have scabby knuckles.

PERSPECTIVE: Did our parents — or any other adults for that matter — know some of the dangerous things we were doing? Probably not.

10

Other Activities

Besides competitive amusements such as described in the previous chapter and in the addendum, we kept ourselves busy in ways that seem really bizarre today. One of the strangest was roasting potatoes — commonly called "potats." This goofy pastime was almost mystically ceremonial in execution. Maybe the reason we didn't do it very often was because over-familiarity would somehow subtract from its neatness B and its inherent weirdness.

A potato roast was a communal effort. The participants would all go home to steal a potato or two from their mother's pantry and meet at[13] the prairie on the corner. After assembling, we would gather some ever-handy firewood and then dig a shallow hole in the dirt using a few sticks and our bare hands. The potatoes were then lightly buried luau-style in the bottom of the hole and the materials for the fire stacked on top and lit. (Mind you now, this was the gourmet recipe. Sometimes when there was not too much planning ahead, the potatoes were simply thrown directly into an already blazing fire.)

---

13 Unlike the real prairies out West, ours was a place to be "at" not a place to be "on."

As the underground potatoes baked we would sit to the smoke-free side of the fire and talk about who-knows-what. I'm sure these conversations were not at all profound — although they could have been. No one went on about the terrible condition of the world (at war), our futures (decidedly grim), or our love lives (not yet started, but predictably also grim). I guess we talked about the Cubs or about the relative merits of some new military aircraft or, more than likely, problems at home. Who knows? In all probability it was just kid talk and no one noticed — or cared — that we had just used a first edition Superman comic book to start the fire.

After an hour or so, or after we ran out of fuel and small talk, the hot coals were kicked aside and the potatoes exhumed. Of course, you know they were done only on one side, but that didn't matter. They tasted great the way they were. No butter, sour cream, or chives. Maybe a little salt along with some dirt, but that was it. It also was a challenge requiring some skill to juggle a really hot potato while trying to eat it without the benefits of any utensils other than our ever-handy pocket knives.

Sometimes our oven timer wouldn't go off and we would leave them in too long and they would get really burned. Of course we would eat them anyway. The charcoal-like outer skin would get smeared on our faces and we looked like victims of a really bad, black face, make-up job.

I really don't know what the fascination was with roasting potatoes, but I'd like to try it again sometime just to see if I could remember how to do it. Today the hard part would be finding a prairie I could use.

Another non-game activity was also carried out at the prairie. This was truly a no-brainer and could easily have led to that condition. Two groups of guys would line up about thirty feet apart and throw rocks at each other! There was no particular reason behind this activity. We weren't mad at each other. It just was something to do, and it made sense at the time.

I am reminded of this scene whenever I see pictures of British soldiers during the Revolutionary War. There they stand, all in nice even rows, shooting at the Yanks. The results were probably similar — the air filled with rocks instead of bullets and hardly anyone getting hit.

We would keep this up for a while, usually until someone did get beaned, then we'd stop, console the wounded and move on to the next event of the day.

One time after we had thrown the same rocks back and forth for a while, a truce was called. At this point I still had a rock in my hand, so, instead of throwing it at the opposition, I threw it up into the air as hard as I could. Sure enough, three seconds later, it came down and beaned a kid. He was bleeding a little, but there was nothing he could do about it. If he went home he'd only get yelled at.

Small manufacturing facilities were scattered throughout many West Side residential neighborhoods. On the next block was a furniture factory that made specialty items out of wood. (During the war they were very busy making coffins for the military.) In the process of building either furniture or coffins, they produced lots of scrap pieces. Several times a day they would dump these little odds and ends into the center of the alley.

These small piles of wood would not stay there long because the wood was heavily prized by the locals for use as firewood to supplement the burning of expensive coal.

The person doing the dumping only had to yell "wood" a couple times down the alley and several little old ladies would rush out with empty bushel baskets to try to snag a share of the spoils. We little kids could not compete with these "wood ladies" even if we got there first. They not only would forcibly take away our little piles but would steal from each other. It was normal to have verbal and physical fights break out over these wood scraps, much to the amusement of the factory workmen who often stood by watching.

During the war, most of the local factories were converted to the production of military supplies. At the end of our block and across the street from the main prairie was the Salerno Butter Cookie Company. Their contribution to the war effort was packaging jellies and jams for GI rations. Each serving of jam was packed in a flat, olive drab tin can about the size of a hockey puck.

As with any manufacturing process, they had rejects which had to be disposed of. These were placed outside on the loading dock for later trash pickup. Once we somehow found out about these "treasures" we just had to have them.

The factory did not have a night shift, but it did have a six-foot tall wooden fence all around the property. We would spy through a hole in the fence to determine if any rejected cans were ready for pickup. If so, we would then scale the fence, toss the stolen cans over the fence, and escape with our hoard.

Big deal, a couple cans of jelly. Nothing we couldn't get at home, but somehow, it tasted better when it was stolen.

All of these activities were total time fillers and were ranked a distant second to the number one, most important thing that we did — alley pickin. This was not only a healthy experience because we had to walk for many blocks, but it was also financially very profitable. Never mind the fact that the total time was spent in the smelly alley.

In those days empty milk and soda bottles were returnable for a two-cent deposit. Finding bottles was the main reason for wandering in alleys and digging through other people's trash. However, it may have been just an excuse, because we would often dig through trashcans even if we knew there were no bottles to be found.

Almost every Saturday morning we would take off early pulling a wagon and cruising the alleys. You would be surprised what other treasures one could find besides bottles.

We got our biggest prizes during metal drives. Periodically during the war the population would be asked to donate metal objects to the war effort. These were collected and, allegedly, melted down to make munitions. (I really do not believe that the metal was actually used for this purpose. The whole thing was probably an exercise to make the nation more aware that there was a war on. A harmless form of civilian participation.)

All sorts of neat things could be "found" on scrap-drive days: lead soldiers, broken tools, metal containers and other treasures which we basically stole from our GIs. I suppose in doing so we could accurately be accused of aiding the enemy's war effort.

I dearly loved to go alley pickin and still have vivid dreams wherein I stumble upon some fabulous hoard of "stuff" lying there in an alley, ready to be loaded onto a waiting wagon.

Another really dumb thing that Bob and I did was to make a zip gun. We slightly bent a piece of copper pipe to resemble an old pirate pistol. Then we padded the handle and drilled a hole where the hammer would be.

The gun was loaded by dropping a firecracker down the barrel so that its wick stuck out of the drilled hole. The rest was simple: stick in some paper wadding, a handful of BBs and more wadding.

We decided to test fire it in the alley (where else?). I lit the wick and Bob held the muzzle out straight, pointing it at a neighbor's garage door about three feet away. It went off with a tremendous blast, put a tight pattern of BBs right through the door and pock-marked the windshield of the car parked inside. We ran away and destroyed the evidence. Who would admit to something like that?

We also would occasionally built things out of the items we found on our alley pickin forays. If we were fortunate enough to find several large pieces of scrap plywood, these would quickly be converted into a makeshift "fort" and set up in the prairie. Because we usually could not find a really large amount of building materials, these structures would be quite small. That didn't matter because the entire construction crew would somehow manage to get inside just before the building collapsed.

By far the best thing to be salvaged from the alley was an old baby-carriage. The wheels and axels could then be attached to some scrap two-by-fours to build a push-cart as shown below.

The driver would sit on the seat, and use his feet to steer by pushing on the pivoted-crossbar in front. Propulsion was supplied by another kid who would push the cart — hence its name.

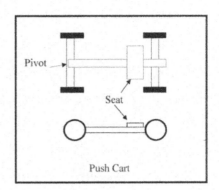

Some parts of Chicago did have slight hilly streets. The kids living in those neighborhoods probably also built push carts, but they could rely upon gravity to enjoy the ride. We were not that lucky.

As it usually turned out, finding the parts and then planning the construction were the most fun. The thrill of riding on the cart — and, of course pushing it — wore out quickly. Also, because of its flimsy construction and rough treatment, the cart wouldn't last very long.

Another construction project consisted of building a wooded scooter. This was a bit easier than the push-cart because it required fewer parts, and they were easier to come by.

The major component of the scooter consisted of a wooden apple box. This item could be acquired from a nearby grocery shop, often by just asking for one.

Back then a load of apples would arrive at the grocer's in a two-compartment box made of flimsy wooden planks. After unloading the produce, the box was usually discarded. It didn't stay in the trash very long before it was "salvaged" by a passerby and used as kindling for the stove or furnace. Whenever we needed one we'd have to be on the lookout and act quickly before some adult came along and beat us to the prize.

Construction of the scooter was very straightforward as seen here. All that was required were two other components: a two-by-four and an old roller skate, both of which were readily available from previous alley expeditions.

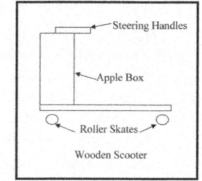

Now that I think about it after looking at the sketch, I can see that our wooden scooter was really a direct ancestor to a modern-day means of transportation — the skateboard.

At the time we didn't realize that there was no need for the apple box. A skateboard would have been so much easier to build — all that was really required was a wider plank and some attached roller skates.

Wow. We were really (almost) ahead of our time and didn't know it.

Oh, well, another opportunity lost.

PERSPECTIVE: I still do miss alley-pickin.

11

Jobs

In addition to the newspaper and grocery store jobs described earlier, I had several serious and even some not-so-serious jobs during high school and college summer vacations.

When I was 16 years old and able to legally get a real job for the first time, I worked at the Fair Store in Chicago's downtown Loop. (The name of the store was derived from the Columbian Exposition of 1893. Unfortunately, it also was a reasonable assessment of the store's quality.)

This was a third-rate department store which had a hard time competing with the really big, first-class establishments such as Marshall Field and Carson Pirie Scott. It disappeared near the end of the early 1980s.

My assignment at the store was in the receiving department in a warehouse located on the top floor of the building. Several of us worked in the women's wear department and our job was to open incoming shipments of dresses, coats and blouses; count them; place them on hangers; hang the items on clothes racks; and deliver the full racks to the various sales departments located within the store.

That job description might sound easy but there were minor variations in the process. Each sales department insisted on a different combination of hangar color, direction of item placement (left or right side facing outward) and rack style. (Okay, that's not very complicated. But, judging from the reaction we got, you would think something really horrible had happened whenever we did it wrong — which was often.)

In spite of being chewed out regularly and having to redo many tasks, I was not fired and managed to retain the job to the end of summer vacation. The experience did teach me a little about the retail trade. But what it really taught me was that I didn't want my life's work to be menial.

The following summer I applied for a job at a metal-stamping company not too far from home. The company was called Poray Inc., a contraction of the Polish owner's name, Mr. Poranski. One of the main reasons I got the job was because I could speak to many of the employees who only spoke Polish.

Most of these people were Displaced Persons (DPs), some of whom were survivors of Nazi prison camps. These individuals were easy to identify: each had a prisoner number tattooed on his wrist. Even though the war had ended years ago and they had been eating well for a while, many of them still looked hollow-eyed and emaciated.

Needless to say, these individuals were eternally grateful to the factory's owner who not only provided them with jobs but also, in many cases, acted as their immigration sponsor and was directly responsible for getting them out of a devastated Europe. I'm sure they worked for minimum wage, but that was far better than anything they could have received in their own country.

My job at Poray was varied. I was an all-around maintenance person. I painted walls, swept floors, hauled trash, helped move and install machinery and, best of all, learned how to drive a forklift truck. The bad part of the job involved occasionally operating a jackhammer — of course, without proper ear protection. Even though I was seldom assigned that task, I did it enough times to permanently damage my hearing.

The following summer I was a high school graduate and could not work because I had to attend summer school to acquire additional math credits to gain admittance into college. As stated previously, it was the last time I had the entire summer off for the next forty plus years.

When the summer following my college freshman year came, getting a job became a serious matter. First of all, I needed it to pay for portions of my tuition and, secondly, for spending money during the next semester. I again applied to Poray and was again hired. This time I was primarily a forklift driver with occasional assignments with the maintenance crew.

One would think because I was older and truly in need of money I would be more serious about my employment. I was not. I felt I was in familiar surroundings and could get away with foolish things.

Since I had more spare time than I needed, I looked for opportunities to play practical jokes on other employees. I didn't think any of these were particularly evil or mean-spirited. Unfortunately, I did not take into account that, because of their very recent prison-camp experiences, many of the DPs had no sense of humor whatsoever.

After a few "harmless" gags (e.g.: ball bearings in the soap dispenser, wash basin water turned off, locked toilet stalls), the floor supervisor met me in the hall, handed me a paycheck for work done to-the-minute, and kicked me out of the building. Really stupid.

But, even though it was the middle of summer, I managed to get another job, even closer to home, at a Motorola assembly plant. I, of course, could not mention that I had completed one year of college because I knew they were looking only for permanent employees, so I said I was a recent high school graduate. I was hired and assigned to work on the police-radio assembly line. My job was to build cables that supplied power to the installed units. It was an easy task that did not take up the entire shift, so during slack periods, I filled in on the assembly line.

I quickly learned how boring this type of work could be. All day long the radio chassis came down a slow-moving belt. At each station we assemblers would grab the chassis, add a few parts to it and pass it on to the next station by returning it to the belt. Even though the belt moved slowly, it didn't stop and there was precious little time between radios. And worst of all, we couldn't dispose of the overflow by eating them as Lucille Ball did in her famous candy-factory sketch.

An interesting aspect of the job is that I had a woman boss who was a real meany. She ruled the line and all of the assemblers were mildly afraid of her.

I really stepped in it early in my "career" when she told me to "Go over there and help those girls." "Girls? What girls?" I asked. "Over there!" she pointed, "Oh, you mean those old ladies." That wasn't very funny at the time, and it endeared me to no one.

Fortunately the "girls" on the line didn't give me a hard time about it and the summer went by quickly without additional faux pas on my part. All in all, it was a wasted summer. I learned almost nothing of value except that I did not want to ever work on an assembly line again.

When I had completed my sophomore year at IIT, many of my peers got engineering-type jobs at several of the high-tech companies located in and around Chicago. I, too, tried to get one of these prized positions but failed.

When asked what my grades were, I was honest and admitted to having a C+ average. I soon learned that an average grade was not good enough to be hired as a summer intern, and to wear a white shirt and tie to the office. I was more the Levis/factory floor type, and I knew it. With that in mind, I applied for a factory job at Zenith Radio which also was located within walking distance of home.

When the personnel guy asked me about my experience, I told him I knew how to drive a forklift. He then asked if I had a driver's license. I, of course, did not have one but made a motion towards my wallet pretending to show him the non-existent document. Upon seeing my positive reaction, he simply said "don't bother" and hired me. I often wonder what I would have done if he had called my bluff.

This was the most satisfying summer job I had to date. I drove my assigned truck all over the plant and loved every moment. I got to practice my driving skills and got paid for my time as well. What could be better?

I soon learned the layout of the place and how all the manufactured piece parts were supposed to move around the plant on their way to becoming a completed product. I soon devised an efficient route, which allowed me to move the largest volume of "stuff" for the minimum amount of effort. I had a great time and almost hated for the summer to end.

The job at Zenith was my last summer job. After that I relied for employment at my fun job; at the Museum of Science and Industry as described in a later chapter.

***

PERSPECTIVE: Each of these menial jobs taught me how important a college education is and, for a while, inspired me to study harder when the next semester began.

There also was a secondary advantage: I now could appreciate what it took to actually build something on an assembly line. This hands-on knowledge became very useful when I became a electronics-design engineer. I always tried to make the job easier for the assemblers and technicians who actually did the grunt work after my designs left the lab and went to the factory.

Besides all that, being a fork-lift truck driver was, and continues to be, the best job I ever had.

12

Schools

As far as we were concerned, there were only two kinds of schools in Chicago — Catholic and public. There also may have been some other religious schools such as Lutheran, Protestant and Jewish schools, but we didn't know about them. And besides, the nuns told us that those people were temporarily practicing the wrong religion and would soon come to their senses. That is what we all prayed for.

Almost every parish had its own small, privately-funded school. Even though the nearest public school was only a block away and could be seen from our front door on Kamerling Avenue, I was sent to a Catholic school located ten blocks away. Not only was this a Catholic school, it was also a Polish-Catholic school — the right kind of school. Its name may not have been very Polish — Saint Francis of Assisi — but a Polish school it was.

There was a great rivalry between the Catholics and the "Publicks." It was the norm to associate only with kids of your type. The nearby public school was named Nobel as in the peace prize. We, of course, showed no respect for this great inventor and humanitarian and referred to the kids that went there as "Nobel dumbbell." They showed equal respect for us by calling us "Cat Lickers."

Even though my fifth birthday was a few months short of the date required at registration, my mother somehow convinced the parish priest to let me enroll in first grade. I don't know if it was done to accelerate my education or to get me out of the house one year sooner. In either case, I can see now that I started school too soon. I was much too immature for the task. I would have been better off intellectually and socially if I had waited a year. But, my mother thought it was a good idea, so off I went.

Although I had to walk the ten blocks to/from school, my home was not the furthest from school. Several other hard-core Polish kids traveled a lot further. We all walked, of course, because there were no school buses and no one knew how to ride a bike. I did not walk alone, however. A big kid (a seventh grader) who lived across the street was paid to accompany me in both directions.

He had a key to our house and often would let himself in and pull me out of bed. Normally my father would wake me and dress me as my mother would be asleep because of her night job. However, after my father left for work I would often go back to bed and have to be forcefully removed by my school guide. Breakfast? Forget it.

As in most grade schools at the time, there was no formal initiation process for the new kids. They were simply picked on by the older kids at every opportunity. The only way to avoid this situation was to become an older kid yourself.

Many first graders, including me, learned some of the ropes (literally) as follows. Our church did not have a belfry. Instead, several large bells were mounted on the top level of a separate, steel-framed structure next to the church. The ropes that swung the bells hung through holes in the roof of a wooded, garage-like building located below the bells. Some of the older boys whose job it was to ring the bells did so only for the pleasure of fooling some little kid into "helping" them ring the bells.

While pulling on the rope, the bell ringer would ask the interested victim if he'd like to help. If the kid said yes, then he would be instructed to "grab the rope real tight when I tell you to." Then, as the bell swung freely and the ringer had the rope pulled down as far as he could, he'd tell the kid to grab it. Sure enough, the bell's momentum would yank the rope up to the low ceiling while the little kid was still holding on. He'd hit the ceiling, let go of the rope, and fall to the floor. Laughter all around. I, of course, didn't think it was funny when it happened to me, but my standards changed when it was my turn to look for bell-ringing helpers.

I attended the same grade school for eight years along with many others in my class. It was a very stable neighborhood and a very stable time even though there was a war going on.

Our school was not in a separate building but was situated above the church. This was very convenient because every school day began in church where the entire student body went to mass. Every class sat (or rather knelt) separately and each was supervised by the ever-present nun. After mass, we all filed out and went upstairs to learn how to be good little Polish-Catholics.

The second floor above the church originally contained eight classrooms. However, a few years before I started first grade, the nuns' house which was located nearby, burned down.[14] The burnt-out basement foundation was left open and unfenced and totally accessible for any kid to fall into — but, for some reason, no one ever did. The site was regarded as a natural extension of our playground area.

Instead of re-building the cloister (it probably was not insured), the pastor of the parish decided to convert some of the classrooms into living quarters for the nuns and to double-up all of the classes. My entire grade school career was spent in four rooms, two years in each.

Some classroom instruction was also conducted in the church itself. Quite often we would take our places in the pews and receive on-the-spot religious training, such as how to: go to confession; receive communion; march in holy day processions; and also, how to become genuine "Confirmed Catholics."

It still bothers me that it was considered normal to teach ten-year-old kids how to "confess your sins." What sins? Many of us had to make things up! But it was all meant to prepare us for when we became adults and could finally do something worth confessing.

The photo at the end of this chapter shows half of the school's entire student body. It was taken in 1943 or early 1944. We were assembled on the front steps of the church/school ostensibly to see the Jeep our parents had "purchased" by buying War Bonds.

_____

14 For some reason, I was not blamed for this fire.

The kids on the right are first and second graders whereas those on the left are from third and fourth grade. The church's Pastor is sitting in the Jeep next to the driver. Note also the two nuns, each of which was in charge of two grades. I'm up front, sitting on the jeep's bumper holding a $25 bond, and my life-long friend Wally is the second kid from the bottom-right of the picture.

Even though the classrooms were on the second floor, the bathrooms were in the basement of the church, and we had to go outside and around the building to get to them. This trek could be used to a student's advantage, as it took a long time for a round trip. While the student was out of class, the subject matter being discussed would be completed and the nun would never know how unprepared the peeing student was. Mostly though, it just trained us to strengthen our bladder-valve muscles.

One kid had a set of very memorable bladder muscles which he cheerfully demonstrated almost on-command. He was the star performer in the bathroom because he could pee an incredible distance! With amazing accuracy, too. I remember how he would often show off his unique talent by standing way back and hitting the porcelain almost every time. None of us could come close, and our futile efforts only added to the bathroom's considerable stink.

Each nun conducted two classes with about 15 kids in each class. Half of the room performed some exercise while the other half studied something else. (It must have been very distracting.) If you were in the odd-numbered grade, you could hear what the bigger kids were studying and kind of get a look-ahead for next year. For the not-so-quick learners, the even-numbered year presented an opportunity to catch up on what was missed the previous year.

Some class material was presented to both sides of the room at the same time. Religious instruction — a major subject — was one of these. The following year, we just heard the same thing again for the first time.

Another major item on the curriculum was Polish. In fact, this was why most of us were sent to this particular school. Quite a bit of the day's instruction was conducted in Polish. Prayers, for instance, were mostly in Polish. Since I only recently converted to English, this was one subject in which I did fairly well.

The other subjects were the usual: history, geography, spelling, arithmetic and the "Palmer Method" of penmanship. From about the fourth grade on, each student's desk came equipped with an ink-well located in the upper-right hand corner. We practiced our penmanship using sharp metal pens that had to be dipped into the ink repeatedly word after word.

What really made this exercise tough was the paper we used. It was of a lower quality than newsprint, very thick and actually had little slivers of exposed wood floating on its surface. How these bits of lumber survived the paper-manufacturing process I'll never know. This blotter-like paper would soak up ink faster than a paper towel if the nib of the pen stopped for even a fraction of a second. That was the challenge: to get through an entire page without leaving a huge blob of ink somewhere.

Ballpoint pens did not come into common usage until the late 40s, and the early ones were very expensive. Their price was beside the point because we were not allowed to use them in school. I got a free one once as a promotional gimmick at a grocery store, and the first time I tried to write with it, the tiny ball rolled out of the tip and the ink oozed all over the paper. I did not recognize this as an improvement in writing instruments.

We did not have PE (Physical Education) because there was no gym or similar facility. Instead, we simply ran around outside during recess. For lunch, the street was closed off with saw-horses and some semi-organized games were played between the curbs and on some neighbors' front lawns. If it rained or snowed, we went down into the musty-smelling parish hall below the church and ran around there for a while. Running around was an important ingredient in all of these events.

Some kids who lived near the school went home for lunch. My house was too far away for the round trip, even when I had wheels, so I brought a lunch from home almost every day. The only other option we had was to go to a tiny store across the street and buy a Twinkie.

Mike's grocery store was typical of the time. It was designed to serve the immediate neighborhood. All of his customers walked there from their homes. It was built on the ground floor of an ordinary wooden, two-story house. Mike lived upstairs and ran the tiny place by himself. It couldn't have been more than twenty-feet square. In comparison, today's 7-11 store would be considered huge.

He sold a little bit of everything — except meats. The shallow shelves were "stocked" with only the products most often used in the neighborhood, and only one or two of each. Because of the severe lack of floor and shelf space, the merchandise had to be stacked vertically, almost to the ceiling. When a customer wanted a seldom-called-for product way up there, Mike used a long pole that was equipped with "grabbers" on the end and either hauled the item down or knocked it off its perch and deftly caught it. (A little free juggling entertainment along with your purchase!) In retrospect, the whole store was really just a large pantry. He did stock Pepsi, Twinkies and Jay's potato chips, so If you only had a dime to spend, why would you go elsewhere?

The absence of formally-educated adults in our house was partially responsible for my not doing well in school. Sure my mother and father were there to help me memorize the Catholic Catechism (in Polish, no less) but that didn't do me much good during Spelling class, or History, or Geography. In addition, their knowledge of math was even shallower than mine. I had to somehow manage my studies on my own, and of course, I did poorly.

I guess I could have gotten help from other classmates. However, kids being what they are, showing any scholastic weaknesses would immediately be translated into a sure sign of mental retardation, and I got enough of that from the nuns. So, I just kind of drifted along doing just enough to keep from being held back, a consequence that was often presented if I did not somehow improve.

I was further hampered by not being equipped with support material such as dictionaries and encyclopedias that were often found in other kids' homes. My dictionary was a thin little thing that caused more harm than good. It omitted many words while taking short cuts to explain others.

For example, when I looked up the new spelling word "gorgeous," I found "see beautiful." What does that mean? Because there was nobody there to explain it to me I failed to understand that it was a directive not a definition. Consequently, if our homework assignment was to write a sentence using the word gorgeous, I would look it up and write "I gorgeous flowers in the garden." Queue class laughter.

At other times, even a massive dictionary could not help solve the mysteries around me. Painted on many fences around the factories in our neighborhood was the phrase "post no bills." What did that mean? I could read every word and even find it in my feeble dictionary, but could not fathom the meaning of the total message. (By the way, none or my friends could either, but they didn't care.) After a while I too didn't care and soon the phrase was either painted over or covered by an ad for a circus or some brand of cigarettes. It was years later when I finally decoded the message "hidden" behind what seemed to me a random collection of words.

One time I came very close to not being promoted to the next grade. It was probably a result of many different events that had happened previously, but the culmination occurred during a class spelling exercise when we were playing a game called "spelling/baseball" (one side pitches a word, if you spell it correctly you take a base).

As the worst speller in the class I often made all three of my team's outs in an inning. As I stated above, no one was available to coach me at home and it's very difficult to teach yourself correct spelling.

In one memorable spelling/baseball game that occurred near the end of a semester, I had already made two outs and the nun was furious. She came out of the "dugout" and took the "pitcher's mound." She said I would be held back a year if I did not spell the next word correctly. The word she selected was "Wednesday," which still makes me nervous whenever I write it. The curve ball part of this word was, of course, remembering to say "Capital W." I was very nervous and stepped out of "batter's box" to stall for time by asking "you mean like the day of the week?" Class laughter. What a klutz!

Well, I got it right, capitalization and all, and moved on with the rest of my classmates. Another crisis averted.

I cannot leave the subject of grade school without mentioning the noble task of "altarboying." This was a pretty neat job and not an assignment and it is described in a later section.

A "privileged" position that I somehow managed to attain was that of crossing guard. To get to school the majority of the students had to cross Augusta Boulevard, a fairly busy street. Fortunately, there was a traffic light there, but if left on their own, most kids would ignore it, and so student-crossing guards were stationed at the intersection before and after school.

We didn't have uniforms but we did wear white belts that not only went around our waists but formed a prominent slash mark from left-shoulder to right-hip. (Kind of like the commonly used not ($\angle$) symbol.)

There were several neat features associated with this assignment: first of all we had to leave class a little early to be at our posts before the rest of the students got there; we also could come in late because we had to be on guard for straggling students; and we learned how to roll the belt into a tight ball that we would then hang from our belts. Needless to say, the last part was the best. A real badge of honor.

By the way; there was no fooling around while acting as crossing guard. Any misstep was met with immediate and severe punishment.

Whenever I mention being punished by the nuns, I mean corporal punishment. Physical! With vengeance! We were pummeled, hit with rulers, slapped and verbally abused, sometimes all at once. And the worst part was we could not complain about this treatment to our parents because the punishment would be repeated at home.

Some of the nuns were truly brutal people who should not have been allowed around children, especially little boys. I've met some pretty sick sisters in my time without realizing it until much later. It was just the natural thing they did, and that was that. And, they got away with it because they had "a special calling from God."

Since World War II was in full swing at the time and my father was too old to get drafted, he had an easier time filling the many factory jobs that were available. The company where he worked had a war-materials contract as did most manufacturing facilities and overtime opportunities — with extra pay — were continuously available. He worked many long hours and I hardly saw him. My mother still held onto her meager janitor-lady job and, being very Polish, they banked as much money as they could.

When I was in either second or third grade, my parents had saved enough money for a down payment on a second house on Crystal Street. This house was located about mid-way between Kamerling Avenue and my school. It was in a newer neighborhood which consisted of long rows of identical two-story brick houses. We moved into the second floor apartment (cheaper) and rented the first floor. Both flats on Kamerling Avenue were also rented. Let the good times roll.

Each house on Crystal had a detached garage in the back facing an alley. Every house and garage was separated by a decent-sized back yard, and along the side property line was a short wire fence with a very loose mesh. The net effect is that, while standing in the back yard, one could see a great distance through all the other back yards. Friends could, and did, communicate by shouting back and forth from yard-to-yard. Who needed a phone?

We did, however, get a phone at that time. It was one of those tall vertical black units with a real "hook" on which to "hang up" the earpiece. It had no dial, so one simply waited for the operator to ask "number puh-le-uz." A true voice-activated system.

Our first phone number was Capital 8297. (Why I continue to waste perfectly good brain cells to store this information is beyond me.) Later, when dial phones became available and the phone company began to move away from mnemonic phone numbers, our number was changed to CA-7-8297. It didn't take a genius too long to figure out that this so-called change was no big deal because the 7 hole on the dial also contained the letter P.

To save on expenses, we initially had a two-party line installed. This meant that sometimes when we picked up the receiver, the other party (some unknown neighbor) could be using the line. When that happened, one simply waited a while and tried again later. Or, you could tell them to get off the line. Still another possibility was to listen in on the conversation. This really didn't make much sense because it usually was in some foreign language like English.

I seldom used the phone to call friends. It just wasn't the thing we did. We just went over to the other guy's house, stood outside and yelled at the front door. Everyone chanted in exactly the same way. If you were calling Bob we would say: "Yo-oh Bob," (pause) "Yo-oh Bobby." Or Bill/Billy or Wall/Wally or even Jer/Jerry. We would keep up this rhythmic chanting until the kid finally answered ("Wha-da-ya want?") or we were chased away by an irritated parent who just couldn't take it anymore.

After my father died we were very short of money even though both my mother and I received monthly Social Security checks and we had three tenants in two houses paying rent. Part of the problem was that rents were under government control and were kept artificially low during and shortly after the War. The properties just did not carry themselves financially.

My mother had always been frugal but now this characteristic went into high gear. Everything was done to conserve money. During the summer we relied upon the output of a small V-Garden[15] in the back yard. This is when I started looking for jobs to supplement the family's income.

---

15 All citizens were encouraged to plant "V-for-Victory" gardens wherever they could to help supplement the food-rationing system.

I bore the entire burden of one of my mother's cost-cutting measures. I had outgrown my only pair of shoes and they began to hurt my feet. So, in order to delay their replacement just a little longer, she cut the threads holding the shoe tips to the soles. Admittedly this did provide some extra toe room but it also let in the rain and my "Charlie Chaplin" shoes further justified my being picked on in school.

But, somehow I managed to graduate along with all the other kids with whom I started school eight years previously. I suspect that many of the things I know today were learned at Saint Francis of Assisi school, but I can't honestly recall any of them at the moment — except, maybe, how to spell "Wednesday."

PERSPECTIVE: It's amazing that a clueless kid like me could actually graduate. Just shows the low level of education we received.

13

Altarboying

When I finally made it to the fifth grade, one of the first things our nun did was ask the boys if any of us was interested in becoming an altar boy. New members were always needed to replace those who had graduated the previous June and fifth graders were the primary source for new recruits. (Of course the question was only put to the seven boys in the class because, in those days, girls were not allowed to assist at mass. Had the girls been included, I'm sure that all of girls would have volunteered as would have all of the boys.)

As it turned out, I was one of the few who did raise his hand. I was not aware that none of the cool guys in the class had their hands up, nor did I notice how surprised/disappointed the nun was that I responded both quickly and positively — a rare occurrence. Normally she would have rejected my gesture for many reasons, mainly she thought (actually, she was positive) that I could not master the many steps involved in becoming a true altar boy. But, because of the otherwise slim list of volunteers, I was tentatively added to the small cadre of recruits.

NOTE: The primary reason the cool guys gave for not wanting to become altar boys was: "I don't wanna wear no dress." The fact that this did not bother me then bothers me now. All I can add in my defense is: we did not wear dresses. We wore cassocks. Big difference? You bet.

Our training was quite simple: we had to memorize about two pages of Latin prayers and learn the seemingly-random motions required to assist the priest during mass. This involved; learning how and when to ring the bells during mass, how to hold and present the water and wine cruets (that was a word I hadn't heard before), and how to light and extinguish the altar candles.

At that point I had been attending mass daily for four years and, honestly, I had not paid much attention to what was going on in front of the altar. I not only had to learn how to perform the various altar boy duties, but also when these duties needed to be done.

Learning how to recite the Latin prayers was our first order of business. If the recruit could not memorize these prayers, there was no reason to go beyond this step. Because I was well-versed in Polish — which is also a phonetically-spelled language — it was easy for me to read and repeat these relatively short, foreign language responses to the priest's much longer prayers. It's strange that we never did learn what each response meant. (Apparently that part wasn't important.)

In addition to learning what to do during mass there were several activities we had to perform both before and after mass. One of these activities was helping our aged — and rotund — pastor get dressed in the vestments he wore during mass.

Before going any further, let me describe our church's behind-the-scenes arrangement. On both sides of the altar were located rooms called sacristies where both the priest and the altar boys got ready for the mass. The altar boy side was on the right (when facing the altar). This was basically a locker room where were stored the red and black cassocks (okay, dresses) and the white, loose-fitting shirts called surplices (okay, blouses). This is also where we hung up our heavy winter coats and hats.

The priest's locker room (sacristy) was larger because it had to hold more religious stuff'. It was on the left side of the altar. After getting dressed, the altar boy (or altar boys, depending upon the type of mass being said) would proceed through a passageway behind the altar to enter the priest's sacristy vestibule and wait while he completed his preparations.

The final piece of ceremonial uniform a priest puts on is called a chasuble. This is a heavy item that looks very much like a poncho that has been decorated with religious symbols. It fits over the priest's head and is kept in place by apron-like ties. The strings to these ties are normally passed behind the back, looped forward and then tied in the front.

As stated above, our pastor was not only old but quite portly. He could not touch his hands behind his back so therefore, he could not execute the loop-back with the apron strings. To help him get dressed, the assisting altar boy had to stand closely behind the priest at the moment he tossed the chasuble over his head and allow it to fall tent-like over his (the altar boy's) head and back. The altar boy would then grab the string ties as they were handed back and switch them left-to-right and right-to-left so the priest could pull them forward and tie them in front.

I'm absolutely certain this procedure was not listed in any altar boy training manual anywhere else except in our little parish.

After the priest had put on all his vestments, it was time to leave the left-side sacristy and proceed out into the sanctuary where the altar was located.

The service always began at the foot of the altar where the majority of the memorized prayers were said. In those days the priest would stand facing the altar with his back toward the congregation, while the altar boys would kneel on both sides of him and responded with our prayer portions. At this point we also had our backs to the audience, so we had to respond loudly to be heard by the congregation. Why did they have to hear us? I don't know. It was all in Latin, which no one understood anyway, but that's the way it was.

During an ordinary mass, the priest would say some prayers and we would answer with a prayer. (In theory, the altar boy takes the place of the people in church and speaks/prays in their behalf.) In between prayers we would be responsible for fetching the water and wine, moving "The Book"[16] from one side of the altar to the other and ringing bells to signal the occurrence of certain significant events. (Some people believed the bell-ringing was done solely to awaken members of the congregation. That could be.)

---

16 This is a large book that contains the prayers that the priest recites during mass. In reality, the prayers have long since been memorized and he just appears to be reading from the book. It's all part of the ritual.

Serving during High Mass was a different matter. First of all a High Mass was reserved for important religious holidays such as Christmas and Easter. During these celebrations not only was the church more crowded but there would be more activity in front of the altar.

Several priests would be in attendance, as well as many more altar boys. Each of us had different duties to perform. In addition, the prayers would be more complex and the audience would see a lot more action. It was a major performance.

During various parts of the High Mass the altar boys had to parade around carrying a cross or lighted candles or a container of holy water. But best of all, they would swing the sensor[17] which was used to lay down a smoke-screen of smoldering incense and thereby enhance the mystical goings on.

All these activities had to be conducted under very strict conditions. No joking or fooling around was tolerated. Hands folded eyes downcast. We had to act as serious as the priest.

In effect, the altar boy and the priest were like actors in a play. We each had our own scripts and had to follow a separate set of stage directions. By becoming an altar boy I had inadvertently entered the world of show business. A religious show, but a show nonetheless.

I also had access to parts of the "stage" not normally accessible to the parishioners and certainly not to the girls. As altar boys we

---

17 A very ornate container that was suspended on chains and was swung gently, pendulum-style by either the altar boy or a priest. Inside the sensor were granules of incense on top of glowing-hot charcoal. This combination created a sweet smelling smoke that was supposed to rise up to heaven — but seldom did.

could boldly walk up the center aisle of the church in full view of whoever was there, open the gate in the middle of the communion rail and walk right into the sanctuary on our way to our locker room. No one else could do that.

The real fun part of being an altar boy consisted of participating in church events other than serving at mass. The two best occasions were weddings and funerals. These ceremonies were emotionally opposite for those directly involved, but most interesting for the altar boys.

Weddings were held on weekends so we had to be pre-assigned to show up and assist the priest. The reward for showing up on our day off was that we'd often get a monetary tip for our services from the groom (or from the best man if the groom was too nervous and forgot).

On the other hand, funeral services could happen any day — but they usually were held on weekdays during school hours. So, not only did we get the opportunity to miss classes, we would often accompany the priest to the funeral home. Sometimes we even went to the cemetery where final prayers were said for the deceased. This meant a ride in a limo, a half-day off from school and, possibly, an after-funeral lunch at a nice restaurant near the cemetery. (No tips, however, but all the other perks made up for that.)

I remember that being assigned to serve at midnight mass on Christmas day was a big deal. This was always a very popular event for the parishioners and the church would be fully crowded. The altar boys would have to get to church very early and prepare for the event. Because this was in Chicago in the winter, it meant riding to church on my bike through either falling snow or through icy ruts of recently-fallen snow. (There were no other options.) But, it was a sacrifice we had to make to get points with God and, more importantly, with the nuns.

I remained an altar boy for the rest of my grade school days and soon became a seasoned veteran. In high school, which was also a minor seminary, I continued to occasionally serve mass for an additional four years. The big difference in high school was I did not have to perform very often because there was a larger pool of altar boys to choose from and my number didn't come up very often.

At this point in my life, I can only remember one of the Latin prayers — the very first response at the foot of the altar: **Ad deum qui laetificat juventutem meam.** It had something to do with thanking God for "giving joy to my youth" — and, in retrospect, I think He did, although I don't ever remember thanking Him.

Even now I have altar boy dreams where I'm pressed to fill the role as an adult. Unfortunately I no longer am a seasoned veteran in the dream. I don't know the prayers nor do I know what to do next and I totally screw things up. But these are happy/funny dreams. They remind me that, at one time, I did manage to learn to do something complex, much to the surprise of my many early detractors.

PERSPECTIVE: I don't know if altarboying did me any good. I'll have to think about it.

14

Bona's

Around the middle of my last year in grade school, a brown-robed Franciscan priest visited our class and gave a slide show to all seven of the boys who would soon be graduating. Several of them had to be forced to attend because they knew what it was all about. As usual, I was clueless and leapt at the opportunity to miss some serious classroom time.

The presentation dealt with a small boarding high school located in southern Wisconsin. It was my first view of St. Bonaventure. (St. Bona's to almost everyone else.)

On the screen I saw smiling students, beautiful grounds, and spacious classrooms. There were also many, many views of the school's chapel, for this was, after all, a minor seminary.

The priest's mission was to entice many of us to enroll in the school and to recruit young seminarians who would then, hopefully, go on to become priests and, like him, join the Franciscan Order.

I had no intention of becoming a priest, but when I saw the pictures I was immediately hooked.

Here I was, about to leave the only school I had ever known, and I still had no idea which high school I would attend in the fall. Although I probably could have gone to any of several Catholic high schools in Chicago, there was a problem: none of these high schools was located close to my neighborhood. To attend any "acceptable" school (public schools were, by definition, not acceptable), I would have to take public transportation. The idea of traveling to and from school on a city bus did not appeal to me at all. It sounded too much like a full time job, and even I was not ready for that.

I soon found out that Wally, one of my classmates, had an older cousin who was a student at Saint Bona's and, furthermore, Wally also intended to apply for admission. After thinking about it for a very short time, my mind was made up. I too would apply for admission. Now, all I had to do was convince my mother to send me.

It turned out that not too much convincing was required. Because the school was heavily subsidized by both the Franciscan Order and through private donations, the tuition at the school was comparable to what was being charged at a private Catholic high school in Chicago. (My monthly Social Security checks would more than cover the low tuition costs.) Besides, it was an opportunity for my mother to conveniently get me out of the house where hopefully I could be taught some discipline. In other words, it was an all around good deal for my mother, and she went for it.

I filled out an application, sent it in, and was accepted. Incidentally, by applying to join a seminary, even a minor one, I scored a lot of points with the nuns and got better treatment for the remainder of that school year.

The nuns had been convinced all along that Wally would become a priest so his status did not improve as much. Incidentally, he did go on to (almost) become a priest. He dropped out at the very last possible moment.

Saint Bonaventure High School was located near Sturtevant, a small farming community in southern Wisconsin. The town is just a few miles above the Illinois border[18] a distance of about sixty miles north of Chicago. The school wasn't really in the town but was situated out in the middle of vast stretches of farmland common to the area.

Even though it was actually quite close to Chicago, the trip took several hours along two-lane roads. (These were the days before interstate highways.) My stepfather Alex didn't want to drive that far just for an afternoon visit, so I did not have the benefit of a pre-enrollment visit. The first time I saw the school was when I was dropped off for my freshman year.

The students' portion of the school consisted basically of two buildings: the older four-story main building and the gym building. (The faculty had a separate building to which I was never invited, so I have no details to report.) The student dormitories, the refectory, some classrooms and the chapel were all located in the main building while the study hall, more classrooms and, of course, the gym were in the gym building. An interesting design feature included a

---

18 A unique feature of this state border crossing was that; located just on the Illinois side were huge signs advertising margarine or "oleo" for sale. Wisconsin was so intent upon preserving its image as an all-dairy state that margarine was not sold anywhere in the state.

tunnel connecting the two buildings. It allowed us to comfortably move between buildings in the rain or following a deep mid-western snowfall.

Our class — the class of '54 — was quite historic. It was the 50th class to enroll at the school since its founding and was, by far, the largest class ever — a total of 100 eager and not-so-eager 14-year-old boys. (Apparently the previous year's student recruitment campaign had been very successful.)

On the evening of our first day a few tearful parents lingered to watch us line up and march into the chapel for the first time. Suddenly, one of boys broke rank and ran crying to his mommy. We were down to 99 students in less than an hour.

Many others left during the first week, and still others transferred out at the end of each semester. New students also appeared each year but, nevertheless, there was a steady net loss until finally, only 40 graduated.

The student body was made up mostly of kids who shared a common Polish heritage. We were the sons of immigrants. Most of our fathers held ordinary jobs in factories and in the steel mills that surrounded Chicago. In many cases, we were the first in the family to enter high school.

We also had a few students from Poland who, themselves, were immigrants. They had survived the war — some in concentration camps — under very difficult conditions. These fellows were glad to be anywhere other than back in post-war Europe.

However, not everyone came from a poor background. Many levels of economic status were represented. One boy was the scion to a family fortune. He was sent to St. Bona's because his second-generation Polish parents felt guilty they themselves did not speak Polish so they sent him away to learn the language. (Needless to say, he was there against his will and not very happy with the experience.)

Another fellow's parents were in business for themselves. His father was a Chicago undertaker. (By the way, meeting this guy proved to be an extremely important event in my life because he eventually became my brother-in-law.)

Rich, poor, smart, or dumb, it didn't matter. We basically were still just little kids, some away from home (and mommy) for the first time. After living in a protected world where someone else always took care of us, we suddenly had to look out for ourselves. No one was there to pick up after us — although there were plenty of people around to pick <u>on</u> us.

No one was there to make sure we had clean socks and underwear. Furthermore, there was no one there to show us how to do all of these things. Each of us had to make the adjustment out of kidhood by himself, a true trial and error situation.

Clean laundry, for example, was each student's responsibility. There were two means by which laundry was done. Some boys periodically sent their accumulated laundry home in specially-designed laundry boxes and got clean clothes back by return mail. (I always thought these guys were momma's boys, but I was secretly jealous of the special snacks and treats that were usually hidden in the incoming packages.)

My mother, of course, would not even consider this arrangement because, first of all, she didn't want to do any laundry at all (including her own), and secondly, the school provided a low cost alternative. Most of the students had laundry done at school by several Brothers[19] assigned to this not-so-wonderful detail. Every piece of our clothing was marked with an assigned laundry number. (My number was 77.)

Located at several places on the dormitory floor were large laundry-collection boxes. The Brothers would periodically collect the dirty laundry from these boxes. They would wash it in a huge laundry room, and fold and place the sorted pile in a cubbyhole assigned to each student. We were then supposed to pick it up on Wednesday or Saturday afternoons, if we remembered to do so.

One aspect of teenage grooming totally removed from our decision process was that of getting a haircut. The big rage in the early 50s was the DA or "Duck's Ass" style of hair combing. To get the look just right, the hair in the back and sides of the head had to be very long so it could be combed straight back from both sides and meet in the middle in a vertical line.

The Administration did not like this look. It was considered "too fast" and not in line with what a proper seminarian should look like. Students who wanted to sport this look had to do it secretly when there were no priests around. Then, when a brown robe appeared, they would quickly re-comb their hair into a more acceptable style. If they did not react quickly enough, the priest would simply mess

---

19 A brother is a member of an order who is not a priest. Although theoretically they are full members, in reality they were treated as inferiors and were assigned all of the menial tasks.

up the artfully-executed DA and order the young trendsetter to go see Bratch.

The word "Bratch" is a modified form of the Polish word "brat," which means brother. Or, in this case, with a capital B which only applied to this one certain Brother. (I have no idea what his real name was.)

He was an elderly man who was not much taller than some of the shortest freshmen. He had emigrated from Europe late in life and spoke mostly Polish and only a little bit of broken English. He was, by far, the kindest and the most gentle of all the adults, priests and brothers, who dealt directly with the students.

One of Bratch's tasks was to wake us up every morning. He would start at one end of the hall and we could hear him approaching as he went from dorm to dorm, ringing a hand-held bell that sounded much too loud for its size. His other important assignment was to give haircuts on Saturday afternoons.

He had a one-chair shop that was so small the student who was next-in-line had to wait outside in the hall while the current victim was being dispatched. He would have done very well in a military boot camp because, no matter what type of cut we asked for, the "baldy sour" was what we got. Bratch just cut it all off, simple as that. The only good thing about the experience was: he was cheap and fast.

As one would expect, most of our day was filled with highly planned, ritualistic activities. To keep order among so many teenage boys, there had to be rules. Lots of rules. There were rules governing just about every little thing leaving no room for either spontaneity, or spontaneous students, as I soon found out.

Most of the students slept in large dormitories according to class year. Each was supervised by a resident senior called a Prefect. Beginning in the sophomore year, two students could share a semi-private room. These rooms were available at a slight surcharge. Wally, the fellow I knew since first grade and I roomed together in our second year and a fellow named Dick and I were roomies in my junior year. Even though the tiny private rooms were just as drab as any of the dorms, they were far superior to the dorm environment. I would have signed up for one in my senior year also, but I was unexpectedly put in charge of a sophomore dorm as its Prefect. This was my first managerial assignment and I failed miserably.

My assigned dorm was the only one located on the third floor, right above the office of the schools superintendent. Because I was basically against the concept of student-administered discipline, I was totally slack with my young charges and we had a very lively time of it. Finally, after a few disruptive months, The Head Disciplinarian could see that this was not going to work out. My dorm was disbanded and all its former residents were moved into other dormitories.

In order to punish and embarrass me for my lack of cooperation, I was not moved into the senior dorm but was assigned a bed in a junior dorm for the rest of the year. Big deal!

The entire student body ate at the same time in the refectory located in the basement of the main building. The room was long and narrow and contained two rows of rectangular tables set on both sides of a wide central aisle. Several priests sat at a long table on a raised dais in the front of the room. (A Brother also sat at the head table and basically acted as a servant to the priests. Many of the students didn't like the idea of this aristocratic presentation but we soon got used to it.)

Students were assigned eight or ten to a table and sat on wooden stools (chairs took up too much room) with the freshman class up front beneath the priests' dais. Each table had an assigned senior in charge who always sat on the aisle facing the raised dais in front.

The seating arrangement for the students was not fixed but was rotated every day. Depending upon one's position around the table, different chores were assigned for that day such as cleaning up after the meal. Each table also had its designated runner who went back to the kitchen to get more food when the initial allotment ran out.

Because of their proximity to the kitchen, seniors could get to the kitchen for second-helpings before anyone else. Some dishes had no seconds: breakfast toast and desserts to name just a few. Now that I can have as much as I want of these foods, I always think of St. Bona's whenever I make more than one piece of toast for myself in the morning.

The food was usually quite tasty and its variety was well beyond my experience at home. I ate it all and seldom complained. Sunday supper was by far the best. The Friday evening meal was the worst because of the meatless restrictions that were being observed by the Catholic Church at the time.

We filed into the room from front to back and stood in silence until after prayers were said. I was among the shortest in the freshman class and sat at the first table located next to the door. Since I always entered early and had to stand while the entire student body filed past me, I would amuse myself by mentally naming everyone in the school as he rushed by. (A total of about 200 student names.)

After I lost this vantage point near the door in my sophomore year, I stopped learning names of the incoming classes and ended up only remembering those in the upper grades, those seated behind me. Every year my list of known student names got shorter.

Some sort of dessert was usually served with supper. Jell-O made a regular appearance as did pieces of fruit and even an occasional scoop of ice cream would top off the meal. These evening desserts were used as a trading/betting medium among students and — no surprise here — they were also withheld from evildoers as a form of punishment.

At the end of every meal the designated cleaner would bus the table; we would recite a parting prayer, and file out to the next scheduled event.

Within the first few weeks of school, I found out why my application was so quickly accepted. St. Bona's did not have very high scholastic entry standards. Naturally, some students were there to become priests, but most of us were not. Some had been given a choice by a juvenile court judge: either reform school or St. Bonaventure. (Some choice!) Several other students were "mentally challenged" and were parked there by their parents in hopes that the priests would somehow help their sons.

And, indeed, most of the students were helped by the discipline, which was strict. Some of us, me included, were beaten often and sometimes without cause. However, since I was used to a similar environment instilled in me by my elementary school nuns, I looked upon these high school thrashings as just a normal extension to my grade school experience.

One aspect of the disciplinary policy I despised the most was the practice of allowing — and even encouraging certain upper-class students to assist the school's disciplinarian in meting out punishment to other students. This task was usually assigned to a few openly-sadistic seniors who had been elevated to the title of Prefect by the administration.

I believe the mistrust of management which followed me throughout my adult working life can be traced directly to my hatred of these individuals. I firmly felt these students were traitors to the rest of us and should burn in hell for their treachery. I still kind of hope I was right.

Those of us who did not conform well (me included, of course) were put on the "DT" list, or detention list, for misbehaving. This was much worse than being smacked because the effects lingered longer. DT duties included cleaning, sweeping, hauling and all sorts of other janitorial-upkeep tasks which helped maintain the school's low overhead budget.

DT lists were posted every Wednesday and Saturday and would take a good part of the afternoon to accomplish. My name appeared regularly, sometimes on several lists simultaneously. I was very popular.

There also were more intense punishments, the worst of which involved missing the Sunday night movie (a truly big loss). In extreme cases, students suffered outright expulsion. A student could be told to leave for any of several infractions, but being caught smoking was the most prevalent. The priests believed in the three-strikes-you're-out rule, and applied it several times each semester.

Any student caught doing something that the administration considered to be evil would simply disappear, often that very same day. The student would be hauled into the Rector's office, his parents would be called and he would be gone. No appeal. No second chance. A very totalitarian society.

One such student-disappearance happened while we were in our junior year's English class awaiting the arrival of our teacher, Father Lambert — who also was the school's Head Disciplinarian. Since the priest was late, we all were naturally goofing around.

The student who sat next to the door acted as a lookout, and when he spied the priest coming down the hall, he came in and alerted everyone by stating (in a much too loud of voice, as it turns out) "Be quiet, here SHE comes."

Well, that was the perfect example of a very poorly-worded statement. As it was, Father Lambert wasn't all that sure of his masculinity and he didn't need to know it was also being questioned by others, especially the students. He was furious as he came into the room, smacked the kid around for a while and led him out of the room.

Even though we knew exactly what was going to happen, we tried to intervene on his behalf. A petition asking for leniency was quickly circulated among the student body, but to no avail. A phone call was made to his parents and he was packed up and gone that afternoon.

Because of my outspoken nature, I was often blamed for the anonymous transgressions of others and suffered innocently. Honestly, I seldom did anything really wrong. I wouldn't dare do anything evil because I was afraid of being kicked out. I knew I had it good there and, if I got the boot, what would I do then? Where could I go?

After being labeled a "dummy" by the nuns and my fellow students throughout grade school, I was amazed to find that, in the transition to high school, the dummy tag I wore had not been solidly affixed and it had somehow fallen off. Apparently, the nuns did not communicate well with the priests and my poor scholastic history did not follow me. (What happened to the old "permanent record" theory?) In high school I was expected to learn things and, if I knew the answer, no one was amazed. I was given a fresh start.

Fortunately, the regimen we followed was very conducive to studying and learning. We had four one-hour study sessions every day, and two more on both Saturday and Sunday. These were held in the study hall on the first floor of the gym building. This was a huge rectangular room that held the entire student body arranged by class from front to rear.

Each of us was assigned an unlocked, flip-top desk in which we stored all our books and writing materials. I brought along my U.S. stamp collection from home which I foolishly kept in my desk.

Within a few weeks, all the expensive mint stamp sets were gone. So much for being good Catholic boys.

We had a half-day of classes on Wednesday as well as on Saturday. The two afternoons were usually free — unless one had to fulfill DT assignments, which I usually did.

We studied the usual high school subjects plus had classes in Polish, Religion and Latin. I did quite well in everything accept Latin grammar. I blame this failure on the way the subject was taught. Latin was presented to us as an integral part of Catholic mysticism not as just another language which could be read and spoken. This approach resembled code-breaking or cryptography: first we learned the rules, then we memorized the meanings of dozens of words, and then we tried to "decode" the underlying messages found in some ancient, non-relevant Roman text attributed to Cicero, or Caesar, or the ever-popular Saint Augustine. It was not presented as an exercise that had any real purpose.

I just didn't get it.

In preparation for the priesthood, everyone had to take Latin for four years, and I fell further and further behind every year. Finally, in my senior year, I decided I would use my study time more constructively: I stopped studying Latin[20] all together because I could see it had no lasting value. Instead, I taught myself something useful — trigonometry. (Trig was not an offered subject but I knew I needed it to get into engineering school.)

---

20 If it weren't for the D grades in Latin, I would have been on the Honor Roll throughout my senior year.

I went to the library, took out a very basic textbook that had answers in the back and then worked every problem in the book. I also bought a 99-cent slide rule through an ad in *Popular Science* and taught myself how to use it. These were, by far, the most ambitious things I had ever done before or since, and I was very proud of myself. Still am.

In our junior year we had a chemistry class and in the senior year, a smattering of physics, both of which I enjoyed immensely. I did have an initial problem with chemistry, however. It seems that my pre conceived ideas about the science were completely wrong.

I thought it was somehow possible to change one substance into another. Just as medieval alchemists tried to change lead into gold, I figured that we would be accomplishing similar miracles. When I learned that chemistry was merely a balancing of equations, and that all the atoms at the beginning of a reaction were accounted for at the end of the reaction and none of them changed into different atoms, it was very disappointing. I wanted "magic" and all I got was a different form of algebra. After I managed to shake off this minor setback, I got straight A's for the remainder of the year — in Chemistry that is.

Our days always started early. At 6 am we were roused by both a fire-alarm type bell and by Bratch ringing his hand-held bell. Half-an-hour later we were in the chapel for morning mass. Then it was off to the refectory for breakfast. The days ended quickly, also. We were in bed each night by 9:30.

Since no one was allowed to return to the dormitories during the day, there were no sessions of teenage napping, except maybe during study hall and, of course, in chapel.

Every day we went to chapel almost continuously. Mass in the morning, a noon prayer session, evening prayers before supper, and prayers before bedtime. We recited our prayers in the world's three major languages: English, Polish and Latin. I knelt so often it took a long time before the flat areas on my knees filled in.

As if the daily routine of chapel attendance was not enough, once every semester we would be subjected to a religious retreat. This was supposed to be a period of serious contemplation and soul searching. (Honestly, what 15-year-old needs to search his soul?)

No regular classes were held during this three-day period nor were we supposed to talk to each other. Nothing earthly was permitted to distract us from our holy mission. No sports, letter writing, or even non-religious studying was allowed. Instead, we attended numerous sermons and were expected to use the time to repent for our sinful past life and to determine our relationship with God and our place in His universe. Blah, blah, blah.

These were very noble goals, but for all practical purposes, unachievable. Oh, of course, we all started out each retreat with the intention of living up to these expectations. But, after the third sermon about "The Role of the Infant Jesus in Your Daily Life," the fervor wore off and our attention drifted elsewhere. It was a nice three-day break from the usual classroom routine, so no one complained.

One of the longest standing traditions of the school was the semi-pagan — well, non-Catholic anyway — rite of freshman initiation which occurred every year around Halloween. This party was sponsored by the senior class with the incoming freshmen as reluctant guests-of-honor. In reality, the two-month build-up and anticipation of the event was more fearsome than the event itself.

The new kids were run through a gauntlet of semi-harmless "horrors" that were organized on the (tarpaulin covered) gymnasium floor. Each event was similar to what one would encounter at a present-day Halloween Spook House. The major difference was we wore blindfolds the entire time. The seniors made us eat worms (spaghetti), drink poison (bitter Kool-Aid), walk barefoot on broken glass (cellophane and eggshells), etc. All this was done with a lot of noise and yelling, and probably a little bit of crying, too.

The worst part of the ordeal was that each kid's face, bare chest, arms and legs were covered with some sort of tarry substance made of molasses, coffee grounds and who knows what else. This stuff was smeared on with a giant brush at the beginning of the initiation and began to dry out as the events wore on. In its hardened state it was practically insoluble and residual evidence of the "tarring" remained behind some unwashed ears for weeks afterward.

I must admit that portions of the event were kind of scary. But I figured they really couldn't hurt us too badly and I was heartened by the fact that, in only three more years, I could partially get even by doing the same to the class of '57. (Funny thing, though, when that time finally came, we had grown a bit physically and mentally and the idea of picking on these little kids was not as appealing as we thought it would be.)

The initiation activities lasted for several hours. At the end of our official "welcoming" to Saint Bonaventure, we had a huge bonfire on the athletic field where we roasted hot-dogs and sang a few songs. That night, I suspect everyone slept well.

I hesitate to bring up this subject, but I feel I must because the question has to have formed in the mind of the reader; given the school's remote location with 200 young boys living with a number of unmarried priests, was there any homosexual activity going on?

I honestly don't know. I didn't see anything, and I surely did not participate in anything. I must admit though that some of the students were, shall I say, a little bit less masculine than others. These guys hung around with each other exclusively and didn't bother anyone else. The homosexual subject was not openly discussed at the time, and no one went into or came out of any closet in my presence.

Many of the priests probably had their own unresolved issues, even though they had already made a life-long commitment to the priesthood. I know of one of our teachers who left the Order and got married soon after we graduated. I suspect that this subject is now handled differently and openly in all boarding schools — at least it should be.

Physical violence among students also wasn't an issue. Oh, there were occasional fights, but these could be classified as mild disagreements. Hardly any escalated to where punches were exchanged. Although I must admit, I did get punched out several times by upperclassmen who didn't understand the cleverness of one of my remarks. Fortunately for me, I have a glass jaw, and the "fight" ended with just the first swing.

One of our most popular indoor sports was also very unique and probably not played anywhere else in the world: picture basketball. Hung all around the study hall were large paintings set in huge, ornate frames each containing a different religious scene. (For student inspiration, no doubt.) Our playing area was at the rear of the room in an open space in front of several of these pictures.

Here we played a form of "one-on-one basketball" using a ping-pong ball. The "basket" was the slot formed between the top of the picture frame and the wall, about seven feet above the floor. It was very hard to hit this three-inch slot, and final scores were usually very low. Most shots taken were hook shots and most scoring baskets were "swishes."

After a player scored, the ball was retrieved by simply pulling the bottom of the picture frame away from the wall so the ball could fall out. I have no idea what religious scenes were depicted in any of these pictures, even though we milled about in front of them for hours. I guess I concentrated too much on trying to dribble a ping-pong ball.

We stayed at school the entire year,[21] except for the summer, and went home only for Thanksgiving, Christmas and Easter, but for only a few days each. Most Chicagoans traveled by rail since the Milwaukee Road passenger train conveniently stopped in Sturtevant. Some lucky guys got a ride home in their parents' cars, but they were the rare exceptions.

---

21 Some students who lived in nearby Racine occasionally went home on weekends, ostensibly for doctor or dentist appointments. But, because there were so few of them, they were the exceptions.

I did not relish going home because there really wasn't much there for me to do. Life was far more interesting at school. One time I got home to find three strangers living in my bedroom. It seems my mother took in this family of displaced persons (DPs) who had recently arrived from Poland and had no place else to stay. Even though it was a kind gesture, it really irritated me because I had not been forewarned and felt like a fool.

To save myself from future embarrassments, I often chose to stay at school instead of going home for holidays. Several other students also did the same thing, so we had the run of the place. We played pool on the senior table whenever we wished, slept late and did not have to go to chapel continuously.

Another reason I didn't like going home, especially for the Christmas holiday, was that students were expected to spend a portion of their vacation time soliciting neighborhood businesses (and even our relatives) to ask them to become sponsors of the school's yearbook.

The impossibility of the task is staggering. Why would any business person from Chicago care to advertise in a yearbook from a tiny school located somewhere in Wisconsin? I hated the role of beggar and failed miserably at this mission. I only needed to try a few times to become convinced that I should never, ever become a salesman.

The school library was small but comprehensive. Several daily newspapers[22] were available as well as many magazines and period-

---

22 What really amazes me is that the newspapers of the early 1950s were full of stories about the Korean War yet none of us seemed interested, even though we were all potential draftees and cannon fodder.

icals. However most of these were religious in nature. What was of particular interest to me was a bound set of *Popular Science* magazines dating back to the early 1920s. I looked through every issue and read many articles, mostly those relating to electricity and electronics.[23] Since students were not allowed to have personal radios, I was primarily interested in finding detailed information on how to build a really small and concealable radio.

Although portable radios were commercially available at the time, they were relatively large and very expensive. They also needed several large, short-lived batteries to operate. The radio I had in mind not only had to be small and hidable, but it also had to operate without batteries. These were tough specifications.

In the older issues of *Popular Science* I found many designs for home-built crystal sets. This primitive form of radio-receiver used headphones and was popular during the early years of radio broadcasting.

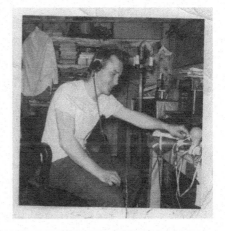

The design was simple, requiring few parts and, best of all, no batteries. There was, however, a serious drawback: they all were built using relatively large components, such as 100 feet of wire wound around an empty oatmeal container.

---

23 Back in the 20s and 30s, the term "electronics" simply meant "radio," since that was all there was at the time.

As time went by and electronic components got smaller, radio designs became more sophisticated and the crystal set became a seldom-seen novelty. After reading both the old and the new articles, I wondered why I couldn't take the old design, eliminate the big bulky parts used earlier, and substitute the newer and smaller components. If that worked, I would have a really small radio that used headphones and did not need batteries.

I put my theories to work during the following summer vacation and the results were spectacular: for a kid, anyway. I took a design that originally could not fit into a shoe box and put it into a cigarette case! I remember plugging in the headset to find that the radio was accidentally tuned to a station playing *"Where is your heart?"* (a song by Felicia Sanders). It was so exiting! I stopped breathing until the song ended. For years afterwards, a strong memory of that feeling would return every time I heard "our song" — me and electronics being played.

So, using the nearby radiator as a ground and my bedsprings as an antenna, I had an operational radio small enough to hide from the "Brown-Robed Gestapo." The down side of the effort was that I would stay up night after night listening to my radio instead of sleeping. The up side was that I knew all of yesterday's baseball scores before anyone else did and occasionally could place a guaranteed-to-win bet with the unwary.

The priests never did find my radio or, if they did, they let it slide. Really, how terribly bad was this? Here was a kid that was showing some kind of talent that, fortunately, was not squelched. In any case, I used it for several semesters then sold it to a kid in a following grade. Sure wish I had kept it.

Television had only recently become available and sets were very expensive. Only the more affluent students had one at home. (Needless to say, I didn't.) The school finally got a TV set when I was a junior. It had a "giant" 19-inch black and white screen and was set up on a high platform in a large assembly room next to the refectory. We were only allowed to watch it on Sunday evenings and then only to view the Bishop Sheen Hour.

The Catholic Bishop of Boston was a very charismatic speaker and, as hard as it may be to believe, actually had a popular weekly network program with national distribution. Not only did we have to watch the Bishop, but we had to pay close attention because his sermon was sure to be the subject of Monday's religion class. Believe me, there wasn't much entertainment value in that arrangement.

Immediately following the Bishop's hour was the Ed Sullivan Show, a popular variety program. As soon as the preaching was over, the students began to plead with the presiding priest to let us watch the next program. Sometimes they would allow it, sometimes not. I guess they figured we were so well grounded in our religious training that we could not easily get corrupted by the "secular world." If only they had known.

In the senior year my study hall desk happened to be in front of the smartest kid in our class. He had always been way out of my league, and we moved in different cliques. Because we were of a different sect, so to speak, we seldom spoke to each other. For some reason, this study period was unsupervised (no patrolling priest) so we could get away with mild conversations.

At that time I was very confused. Graduation was at hand and I didn't know what I would do with myself. At the same time, I wanted to know what a really smart guy was going to do. I turned to him and asked "what are you going to do after graduation?"

His response was stunning:

I believe that the nations of the world will soon be moving into space, and in order to do so, special materials will be required to build the spacecraft. Because of this I plan to become a ceramics engineer.

Good grief, a ceramics engineer! I had no idea what that even meant. Here was a guy who had his future (and the world's) all figured out at the age of 18. Listening to him was truly a humbling experience which put me on guard and in my place. Is this what he and the other class "intelligentsia" talked about? No wonder he didn't run around with my duffus crowd. If he represented my future competition[24] I was doomed. How could I ever make it in the technical world?

In spite of this mental setback, I decided to try to get into engineering school anyway. The trouble was I did not know how to go about doing so. Since the school's idea of "Career Counseling" was limited to trying to convince students to become priests, I had to

---

24 I met up with this fellow years later at a class reunion. He, of course, did not remember the conversation that made such a big impact on me. I learned that he had enrolled in an engineering school with the intention of becoming a ceramics engineer. But he found the course work too difficult and he did not graduate. When we met, he was working at a department store selling children's clothes. My competition had dropped out of the race early and I didn't even know it.

seek help elsewhere. I knew that our physics teacher had graduated from Illinois Institute of Technology so I asked him for help.

Because IIT was located in Chicago, I figured it was the only place my parents could afford to send me. He showed me how to send away for an application form and a class catalog and told me what to do next. Also, since I could not take an entrance exam because of my location, the test was sent to him and he proctored me while I took it.

I passed the exam and was conditionally accepted: (I had to attend summer school to take an advanced algebra class.) My self-taught knowledge of trigonometry, however, proved to be adequate and did not need to be repeated. How about that!

Near the end of our final semester all seniors were subjected to an exit interview conducted in the Rector's private office. Each of us was ushered in, one at a time (in alphabetical order, no less), and asked to sit in a huge chair opposite his enormous desk while he asked questions dealing with our plans for the future.

Each interview lasted about 10 to 20 minutes while those next in line waited nervously in the hallway. As a guide to his series of questions, he referred to a stack of file cards each student had completed at the end of each semester.

These cards contained a series of highly biased, YES/NO questions such as: "Are you interested in becoming a priest?" "Do you want to become a priest?" and "Do you believe you are well suited to becoming a priest?" The only one missing was "Do you want to go to hell for not becoming a priest?" I, of course, responded NO to each of these leading questions on all of my cards.

As I walked into the office, the Rector quickly thumbed through my eight cards and reached a conclusion even before I could sit down, he said "That'll be all." I stopped, turned and walked out. The dreaded interview lasted less than five seconds, an all-time record never to be broken.

My quick departure really amazed the guys waiting in the hall and was the topic of conversation for several days.

The months before gradation were tense, filled with teenage apprehension as to what would follow. Then, when the day finally arrived, we got through the ceremony quickly and acted very brave by pretending that leaving the school was no big deal.

However, we all knew it was a big deal and the good old days were truly over. We piled into our parents' cars and got out of there quickly for the silent ride home.

What was wrong with us? There we were, teenagers in the 1950s, for God's sake! The best combination of events there ever was. Times were good. Unemployment was low. American cars were big and shiny and all teenage girls were beautiful. Unfortunately, I didn't learn to appreciate these conditions until much later when I watched Fonzie on "*Happy Days*" and privately wondered why I had been given a different script to read.

During the summer months following graduation I attended St. Philip High School in Chicago to take the requisite algebra class

I needed for entry into IIT. Although I didn't necessarily want to go to school after graduating, there was one advantage to this arrangement: I didn't have to get a job for the entire summer. I had no way of knowing it at the time, but 45 more summers would quickly pass before I could again make that statement.

Saint Bonaventure went through major changes after we left. A year or two later the main building burned down and was replaced by a sleek, new structure that looked nice, but just wasn't right.

Interest in the priesthood had also been on the decline for many years and really began to crash in the early 60s. Consequently, student enrollment continued to drop until the level became unsupportable. Finally, local day students were admitted to help meet expenses, and that killed the whole idea. Operations had to be suspended, the students were sent home, and the place was put up for sale.[25]

It has often been said that "you can't go back" and, in the case of Saint Bonaventure, the saying is absolutely true. The school is now just a memory to hundreds of not-so-young "Bona Boys" whose number continues to diminish.

PERSPECTIVE: There is so much that I owe to Bona's. Not only did it get me away from my continuously-fighting family and crummy neighborhood, but it also taught me that I was not a complete dummy. I'm absolutely certain that if I hadn't gone there, my life would have ended badly — and probably much sooner.

---

25 Mercifully, the state of Wisconsin bought the property quickly and converted it into a prison. Comments dealing with this conversion are self-evident and have not been included.

15

IIT

After attending school for 12 years under fairly sheltered conditions, I finally entered the big world. I soon realized two things (1) I was not prepared for the big world, and (2) I had not planned my schooling correctly — I did it in reverse. Instead of going away to college as is the accepted norm, I went away to high school and came home for college. At the time I didn't realize I had done it wrong, so it was no big deal. I was more involved with the fact that I was the first member of my extended family to actually go beyond high school.

My other big school-picking mistake was that I attended a high school not only far away, but it was a seminary — all boys, no girls. My college selection may have been even dumber. It was basically an all-technical school which meant the student body consisted of hundreds and hundreds of techno-weenie guys and, of course, no girls.

I must admit there were a few girls enrolled at the school, but these were young women who were interested in having careers in chemistry, physics and math which immediately meant they were "non-hot." As far as I was concerned, their hotness rating didn't matter since I had no experience in dealing with women anyway.

As with many incoming freshmen, I was overwhelmed with the size of the school and the magnitude of the student body. For example, one of my first classes was CHEM101. It was not held in a classroom but in an auditorium, and there were more students enrolled in this one class than there were in my entire high school.

I also was not prepared to make all the choices expected of me, such as selecting classes and buying books. This was all new to me. There were no such choices to be made in high school. Each of the four grades had its own classroom and all the students were assigned the same schedule.

I had no idea how to register for classes and didn't even know which classes I was supposed to take. And, worst of all, I knew no one and didn't know where to go for advice.

Even though each incoming freshman was assigned a senior "big-brother," I could never find him. But that really didn't matter much because even if I did find him I probably wouldn't know what to ask him. The bottom line was: I absolutely didn't know what I didn't know. It was a rough start.

Back in the 50s, IIT was a relatively small school, but it was growing very fast.[26] The aging facilities were woefully inadequate and could barely accommodate the existing student body, yet more and more students were being admitted each semester.

---

26 The Administration liked to compare the school against the real giants in the field such as MIT and Cal Tech. Unfortunately, it was not a successful comparison. Also, "We're number ten" was not a very catchy motto.

When I enrolled as a freshman in 1954, the "missile gap" with Russia had not yet been recognized much less named. However, we all knew the country had an engineering shortage because it was continuously written about in the papers.

The nation was coming out of the glory days following WWII, and the editorials kept telling us only good things lay ahead for everyone, and especially for those who graduated from a technical school. I really wanted to be counted among that crowd even though I really had no idea what an engineer was supposed to do.

The school was essentially a commuter school catering mostly to Chicago residents. Although there were some fraternity houses on campus, they were not besieged with requests to join nor were they very influential in school politics. It seems technical people, even students, tend to be non-joiners. Consequently, the GDI's (God-Damn-Independents) were the strongest majority on campus.

The campus was/is located on the far South Side of Chicago at 33rd and State Street. Since it would be a while before I had access to a car, I had to travel by public transportation.

The one-way trip took about an hour. It involved a long bus ride to downtown followed by an even longer ride on the subway/ EL, followed by a long walk — always into a stiff north wind — from the 35th Street station.[27] Getting to school in time for an eight o'clock class in the winter was quite a challenge.

---

27 The southbound EL trains did not stop at 33rd street in the morning even though there was a station there. The northbound "B" train did stop for passengers during the evening hours. Never did understand why the school did not have enough clout to change this situation.

Luckily for me, I came equipped with some disciplined study habits derived unknowingly from Bonas. My first semester went well. I studied hard because I had no distractions (meaning: no social life) and got a B+ average. I felt good about it.

I soon met up with a cast of characters who improved my social life but stomped my scholastic life. Frank and Flo[28] (a couple of guys I met at school) introduced me to the Museum of Science and Industry and I began to work on the school's weekly newspaper. These activities started out as small diversions but quickly grew and grew. Soon they began to use up most of my time until very little was left to devote to schoolwork.

I must admit I really liked being part of the school's newspaper staff and being able to hang around clever people. I also reveled in the excitement of putting together a newspaper. (Cleverly named *The Tech News*.)

The staff was small and we all pitched in to do a bit of everything. Up until that time, I didn't realize how much effort was involved in producing even a small weekly newspaper. I was a proof reader, a reporter, and the sports editor. I even wrote phony letters to the editor and then rebutted them on the editorial page. We did anything we could to fill column space.

But I had the most fun was while co-authored a weekly humor column under the byline "Tonto and Kemosabi." (The other guy was Tonto.) Our specialty was writing original little stories (we called them "Fables") that ended in a distortion of a commonly-used

---

28 Although Frank and Flo (Florien) were two distinct guys, they were always seen together and, for all who knew them, the phrase "Frank-n-Flo" became a single word.

phrase. ("He who lives in a grass house shouldn't stow thrones" was one of our best.) Some of these were very clever and the really good ones were often stolen and reprinted in other college publications — the sincerest form of flattery.

The staff did spent a lot of time together and even formed a bogus fraternity. It was called the "White Rooks." The name was a take-off on the most elite campus fraternity which was named the "Black Knights." This was a technical fraternity which recruited only the best and smartest students. The White Rooks were a lot less picky.

The newspaper crowd was not always immersed in printer's ink. We also spent a lot of time at a local tavern trying to immerse each other in cheap beer. Five or six of us would often set out for the Three Deuces (named after its address — 222 West 33rd Street) intending to finish all our columns in the back room. This seldom happened. We would end up doing nothing more than drinking Drewry's Ale and playing Liar's Poker all afternoon. Late sessions at the Deuces plus working at the Museum on weekends began to fill my schedule.

It's no big surprise that something had to give. And it did — my schoolwork. All grades began to slip until I was put on scholastic probation in my sophomore year. This meant I was restricted to a smaller class load and was not allowed to participate in any extracurricular campus activities.

I willingly accepted the concept of taking fewer classes because that gave me more time to hang around with the newspaper staff. I defied the extracurricular activities ban by taking on the pseudonym/pen-name of Phil Marz and continued writing for the paper.

The combination of smaller class load and failed grades caused me to slip even further behind. Even though it was 1957 and I was in the middle of my fourth year at school, I was still more than a year's worth of credits away from graduation. It was a tough climb, but I was sure I somehow was going to make it. Obviously, I could not graduate along with the rest of the class of 1958, but hopefully, sometime soon.

Then it happened. The Russians launched their little Sputniks and all things technical went crazy.

Suddenly, the U.S. was forced into entering both a space race and a missile race. The newspaper editorialists wrung their hands daily about how far the U.S. had fallen behind and how hopeless our situation was. I thought this state of affairs may actually be a good thing for me because, if engineers were really needed, then hiring standards might come down and I could actually get an engineering job somewhere.

I had that figured all wrong. From my perspective, it was a complete reversal of thinking. Technical schools began to tighten their standards not only for admission but for student retention. To make room for the more-qualified incoming students — the ones who really could save the country — all poor performers had to be removed. That was me.

At the end of yet another not-so-particularly bad semester (for me, anyway) I was summoned to the Dean's office and notified that I would no longer be allowed to attend day classes. After 15 years of being threatened with expulsion by both nuns and priests, it finally happened — I was kicked out of school, and by someone wearing a business suit instead of a black habit or a brown robe.

What to do, what to do?

I certainly did not want to change to an easier, non-technical major, so I knew I had to somehow graduate as an engineer. Half an engineering degree was of little value in the job market so I kept my weekend Museum job, said goodbye to the newspaper crowd and enrolled in night school the following semester.

I had been properly humbled.

Although night school was a grind, it exposed me to an aspect of engineering I had never seen. In day school, the concept of engineering was presented as a theoretical exercise. None of the professors (in most cases, only graduate students) had ever held "real" jobs. They had no idea what the real world applications were for the material we were required to memorize from our textbooks.

In direct contrast, night school classes were full of real engineers. Most of the students — and even some of the professors — had real day jobs solving real engineering problems. Sometimes they would introduce these real-world, day-job problems to the class as examples of what was going on "out there." This true learning experience combined with my sorry situation rekindled my enthusiasm for learning and for getting the hell out of there.

I also discovered that I had finally outgrown the museum experience and needed to get a job that paid some real money.

Ralph, one of my IIT classmates, graduated on time and immediately got a job at a telephone-manufacturing outfit called ITT/Kellogg. He told me he was not only having a good time being an engineer but that the work was very easy because everyone was working on government contracts. (Some things never change.) In spite of my non-degreed position, Ralph suggested I apply for an engineering job at his place of employment, which I did.

As I had hoped, the Company was desperate for technical help and I got a job, but it was not in a true engineering position. My job was in the publications department writing technical manuals. Turns out I was hired because of my school-newspaper background so something good finally worked out.

One real benefit of this job was the company paid the full tuition for all undergraduate classes. I continued to be subsidized in this manner for two and a half years (summers included) while attending night school and finally graduated in 1960, six years after leaving Bonas.

In night school I got all A's and B's, but my overall grade point average did not rise substantially above a C- because of the early years of neglect. I did, however, manage to get my overall up to the absolute minimum required for graduation. (I still take pleasure in claiming to have graduated in the top 100 percent of my class.)

The sad part about my graduation was that neither I nor my mother was able to attend the diploma ceremony. (She really wanted to see her son graduate and actually receive a diploma on-stage. I guess I did too, but it was not to be.)

I had signed up for a stint in the Marines and had to report to boot camp in early June, a few days before my final exam. I believe he professor took pity on me and allowed me to take the final as a take-home exam. I don't know if I did well on the test or not, but he gave me an A for the class, probably as a patriotic gesture.

After six years of schooling, the diploma arrived, unceremoniously, a few days later by mail.

After working for many years as an engineer, I again enrolled in night school, this time at UCLA. It was gratifying to learn this time I was viewed as one of the "real" engineers by the younger students in the class.

The courses I took at UCLA made a profoundly positive effect upon my engineering career and, consequently, the rest of my employed life. These classes all dealt with computer design, logic and programming, none of which even existed as courses of study just a short while earlier at IIT.

PERSPECTIVE: I now feel embarrassed to have made so many poor choices as a college student. I suppose these were due to a combination of immaturity and unfulfilled social needs. Consequently, it has always been difficult for me as an adult and even as a parent to advise anyone on how to behave because I certainly did not present a good example when I was younger.

16

MSI

Shortly after I met Frank-n-Flo (remember them?) during my sophomore year at IIT, they told me about the interesting weekend jobs they both had at the Museum of Science and Industry (MSI).[29] They no longer worked at the museum but often related numerous stories about the fun they had and about all the hot young college-aged women who were still employed there. In other words, meeting babes was the real purpose of the job. The (low) pay was almost incidental. This I had to check out.

I had never been on a serious interview before, so I talked my friend Ralph into going with me and also apply for a position. We made an appointment and went on the "EL" one day after classes.

We started our trip from IIT, which already was on the South Side of the city and it still took a very long time to get to the museum located even further south. And, since we both were "Northsiders"

---

29 It was, and still is housed in an huge Greco-Roman style building that served as the Palace of Fine Arts during both the 1893 World's Columbian Exposition and during the 1933 Century of Progress Exposition.

and had no cars, the prospect of riding public transportation that far just to get a low-paying job was a real turn off. But we took the interviews, got the jobs and thought we would give it a try in spite of the long commuting distances involved.

We soon learned that Frank-n-Flo were right about the low pay ($1/hr) and semi-right about the babes (just okay). Most of the lecturers/demonstrators were my age, they attended school during the week and worked at the museum only on weekends. It was a real partying group and we easily spent more money than we earned each weekend.

The problem Ralph and I had was that almost everyone else who worked at the museum was a Southsider. So, if there were any late-night after-work activities, he and I did not get home until very late. At the time, I was taking a full load of classes at IIT as well as working on the newspaper staff. I already had enough distractions, and the museum job only added to my list of excuses not to study. I didn't care. I could always catch up next semester. Yeah, right.

All the staff wore uniforms and we were assigned posts throughout the building on a semi-random basis. In some exhibits we were required to give periodic lectures. In others, we simply acted as low-paid security guards.

My first assignment was to give tours on the submarine.[30] This was a very tedious position, but we all had to do it because it was a kind of an initiation rite for all new recruits. In summer we gave the

---

30 For no apparent reason, the museum has on-display a German U-boat captured during WWII. Even though it has nothing to do with either science or industry, it continues to be a popular and profitable exhibit.

same 15-minute lecture dozens of times a day, almost without a stop. The only time we could rest and socialize was between tours, and that was only for a few minutes. This was when we would proudly share our brilliant comebacks to the sincere (but dumb) questions posed by the visitors. (It was all quite amusing at the time.)

After apprenticing on the submarine for a few months, Ralph and I were assigned to the Electric Theater. Now this was show biz! This I liked!

Ralph and I would alternate giving a half-hour lecture on a real stage to a seated audience of about 200 visitors. On stage we would demonstrate many aspects of electricity, energy, light and magnetism. One of us would lecture while the other was in the wings operating the lights and controlling a few on-stage gimmicks. Although the script was supposed to be rigidly fixed, we often improvised either the contents or sequence of the material just for variety's sake or to suit the audience. This was a true learning experience which helped me get a technical-instructor job and also to teach at a community college.[31]

I also spent many days at the information desk located in the middle of the entrance foyer. I liked this spot because it was a power position and I had access to a lot of dumb questions plus it provided an opportunity to respond with witty retorts,[32] most of which were wasted on the unwashed public.

---

31 During the interview I was asked if I had ever spoken in front a large group before, and I replied "never to more than 200 people at a time." Got hired on the spot.

32 Some visitors confused MSI with Chicago's Field Museum where Egyptian mummies were on exhibit. Consequently, we were often asked "Where are the mummies?" To this I would sometimes respond, "In the basement and ten miles north." Hilarious!

As usual, my reputation as a "funster" got me into trouble with the management. In many instances other people would pull some stupid or outrageous prank, and I would get blamed for it. The situation was reminiscent of my high school experience, except I did show some progress — at the museum I didn't get beaten.

A classic example of misplaced blame involved an incident that happened in the medical section of the museum. The displays there were designed to show how science is involved in the field of medicine. Among other items on-exhibit were several miniature dioramas that depicted different operating-room procedures and how they had changed over time.

One of the guys managed to pick the lock on one of these tiny dioramas and then rearrange the nurse and doctor dolls into a very compromising position on the operating table. I suspect that most visitors thought this doctor/nurse relationship was normal because the changes were not reported to management for quite a while. But, when the word got there, I was one of the few who were interviewed (grilled, actually) in a failed attempt to find the culprit. We all knew who did it, but because we were extremely loyal to each other, no one snitched.

We also had a practical joke that we pulled on newly-hired people. It involved the Foucault pendulum. This exhibit demonstrated that the earth did, indeed, rotate about its axis. To do so, it employed a heavy pendulum suspended on a long line over a clock-like surface marked with hours of the day. The pendulum was set in motion every morning at opening time (9 am) and, as the day progressed, the earth would rotate under the pendulum, and the pendulum's back-and-forth motion would slowly shift to indicate the time-of-day.

The practical joke part was to send the new guy looking for what was called "the pendulum wrench" which was allegedly needed to adjust the system whenever daylight savings time went on or off. (Of course there was no such adjustment required because the pendulum was always started at 9am no matter if we were in CST or CDST.[33])

In retrospect, nothing extraordinary happened at the museum, and the few episodes that did occur seem very trivial today. However, we were kept on a constant "high" by a lot of little events. A stupid question from a visitor (plus our witty retort, of course) would be repeated over and over again. And the sad thing was we thought it was just as funny every time. I guess we were all starved for companionship and the place provided a kind of secret clubhouse-atmosphere we all lacked in our lives.

Ironically, even though many of us were there for mutual companionship and human interaction, most of the exhibits were solitary postings, with just you and the visitors. The only time we saw one another was during break periods. Somehow, this was okay as long as there were after-work activities to make up for it.

Almost every Saturday after we turned off the lights we would head out in a mob to a movie, restaurant, comedy club, or to a jazz-joint. At other times there was a party at someone's house. It was all

---

33 It's a bit complicated, and I'm sorry if you don't get it. This was truly an insiders' joke.

just a group of friends, sharing time together. There was very little pairing-up going on, and the couples who did went off by themselves.

Sometimes the gang would go to a mildly expensive restaurant and run up a huge bill. Then, when it came time to pay, everyone would throw in his under-calculated share of the check and would quickly leave. Several times I did not manage to get out the door fast enough and got stuck with the considerable balance-due. To this day I continue to be wary of any "let's split the bill down the middle" arrangement.

Ralph and I didn't have parties at our houses because first of all, we lived so far away. And, quite frankly, our homes were shabby compared to those we visited. Also, most of the others lived in single-family homes in the near suburbs while Ralph and I were city dwellers who lived in multi-family apartment buildings. These were big differences from both a social and economic perspective.

One year I got the brilliant idea that Ralph and I should somehow re-pay all the people who had invited us to parties at their homes. We decided to rent a bar and throw a private New Year's Eve bash. This was a very cool idea and it cost us a considerable amount, but at the time we were both working at real, full-time day jobs so we could afford it. As it turned out, it was well worth the expense.

Another thing I could afford at that time was membership to the Playboy Club. (At that time only one Playboy club existed and that was in Chicago.) I became a charter member soon after it opened and would go there more often than I should have.

It was a really neat place. Every member had a charge account and everything had the same price, $1.50 — drinks, beer, cigarettes, pool games, lunches — everything. (I don't know what else was on-sale there because it didn't occur to me to ask.)

One North Side joint not too far from my house that we frequented was called "The Scene." Admittedly a very corny name today, but at the time it was very hip. They had a live jazz band almost every night and the best part was I didn't have to travel very far to get home and crash after a visit.

All of our innocent adventures were occurring while the Beat Generation was in full bloom. Some of us were very taken up by the concept. One of my IIT newspaper guys was especially influenced. He got into the habit of putting some strange looking leaves into his brandy-filled hookah and just kind of drifted off.

I did not completely join "The Beat Generation." I did, however, buy a cheap guitar and even took some lessons. I would also write some heavy, dark Beatnik poetry B especially when I was feeling sorry for myself, which was often. Once, on a dare, I got up in front of the patrons at the Pink Pig, strummed a few chords on a borrowed guitar and recited my deepest, darkest (and shortest) poem:

"Be gay".
You say.
"Life's swell"
Hell!

I got some mild applause (finger snaps, really) and sat down. That was it for me and show biz. I still think it's a cool poem, but unfortunately, it's meaning has been radically changed by time. ("Gay" was a perfectly good word back then and had no secondary meaning.)

I had several different employment relationships with the museum: I worked there part time on weekends while I was a student at IIT; also as a full-timer when I was kicked out of day school; and again as a part-timer after I got a real day job. I had been there far longer than most people stayed and it just wasn't normal. Almost all of those who were working there when I started were gone, and when new members joined the staff, I didn't even bother to learn their names. It was plain for all to see that I had overstayed. The time had come for me to let go. Leave the nest and get on with it. That was a scary concept to face.

At the time we were certain that all of us who worked at the museum were normal guys and girls. Now it is easy to see we all had many problems, social and otherwise. Very few of us knew where we were going in our careers nor did we know if we even had careers. We also knew we should be getting ready to go out into the real world and that we were very much unprepared for the journey. The museum provided a convenient rest-stop at the beginning of an uncertain road which was opening ahead of us. I'm so grateful to have had a membership in the MSI clubhouse at a time when I needed it the most.

As mentioned above, we had lots of "free" time while tending our assigned exhibits. I spent some of that time studying but I also did some writing about this and that in a spiral-bound notebook. I also continued documenting my feelings in that notebook long after I left the museum.

Years later while going through some boxes of books and things I happened to find that long-forgotten notebook. The diary-like entries dealt with my misgivings about my life, my uncertain place in the world and how unhappy I was with my surroundings. But mostly, it dealt with how unhappy I was with myself.

The notebook contains about 40 pages of handwritten outpourings, most of which were written while I still worked at the museum. Some were written in ink, others in pencil and often on both sides of the paper — which made some of the entries hard to read because some of the writing had bled-through from one page to another. Nonetheless, I did read all of the entries in that diary/journal.

Hardly any of the pages captured anything positive. They were all about my many failures in school, lack of money, friends, girlfriends and basically, a total lack of prospects for improvement in any of these categories. It's no wonder I was in such a miserable mental state. I was a real loser!

And rightfully so. I was living at home in a really horrible part of town. Fighting constantly with my mother. No car, no money, no job, kicked out of school. Man, it's surprising the last entry in the diary doesn't end with a suicide note. Reading those scribbled comments made me feel really sorry for the screwed up, twenty-two year old who turned out to be me.

Did I learn anything by reading those pages? Probably only that I'm glad I had the sense to write down my feelings. Otherwise I had no other outlets for them and keeping them covered could have lead to a far less desirable result.

I was also surprised that, as a young person, I took the time to write such a large volume of personal material. It apparently was a very useful emotional outlet. Even though it took several years to fill the notebook, it is an impressive work.

One portion that says a lot about my life occurs at the very end of the notebook. The narrative suddenly ends with some nervous thoughts about getting married in a few weeks, and that's it.

The last few pages are blank! In other words, I did not return to fill those pages with more negative entries simply because there were none. The book was closed because my life got better from that point onward!

I always thought this was the case and now I had documented proof.

PERSPECTIVE: Even though it was a real workplace, the museum served as my clubhouse. Working there forced me to become aware of social issues; how to talk to strangers; how to deal with girls; how to stop being a kid. These experiences served me well in my adult life — which was scheduled to start shortly thereafter.

17

USMC

Shortly after graduating from high school I turned 18 and, along with millions of other guys the same age, I had to register for the draft. My draft board (there were many throughout the city) was located near the corner of Pulaski and Madison, a seedy neighborhood then, a really dangerous one now. It only took a few minutes to sign up. All we had to do is show some sort of identification. Mine was my birth certificate (still no drivers' license).

A few weeks later I was notified to report to a downtown armory for a physical. This proved to be an interesting/weird, all-day experience.

It seemed to me there were hundreds of us, although it was hard to judge numbers with all the milling around. We were poked, examined and tested, but mostly just waited for the next round of poking, examining and testing. After a full day of this routine I was convinced military life was not for me and I should avoid it if I could, but how?

Just before we were finished with the physical we were each handed a heavy brown envelope containing propaganda literature about each of the military services and why we should enlist in any one of them. As I headed for my bus stop just outside the Armory I noticed a conveniently-located trashcan. I quickly lobbed the envelope into the bin. That's when I noticed it was about half-full of unopened, identical, brown envelopes. So much for the allure of military recruitment.

A few weeks later I got my draft card. I was 1-A, the first to go.

Six years went by and I heard nothing from Uncle Sam. At that point I was in my final semester at IIT and on the verge of graduation. If Sammy wanted me he still wasn't saying so. I did figure my number would be up shortly and I had to do something about it if I didn't want to get drafted into the Army.

I learned through some guys who worked at the museum that there was a program in the military called the Critical Skills Program. This program was not widely advertised, and it was easy to see why. In fact, it was a semi-secret, even at the draft board.

The object of the program was to keep critically-skilled employees on-the-job instead of in-the-trenches. At the time I was working in the publications department. In reality, this was not considered to be an engineering position so I really didn't have a "critical" position or even a "skill." However, some of the company's contracts were part of the Atlas Missile program so I technically did qualify, but just barely.

It took a while to get the forms from the draft board because, at first, the people there denied the existence of the program. However, after some insistence, the forms were found and filled out. Among the items asked for was a listing of all the military contracts I was working on and an authorizing signature from the company's personnel department.

In a few weeks — surprisingly fast for a military bureaucracy — I got my deferment. However, it presented only a temporary reprieve. I still had to put in my time somewhere in the military. Mercifully it would consist of only 90 days of active service instead of the standard two year enlistment.

Following the active duty portion was a mandatory period of eight years in the standby reserves. This membership did not involve monthly meetings or annual camp-outs. All I had to do was continue being qualified as a critically skilled employee by working for a company that had a military contract. Since that is what I wanted to do anyway, it was no big deal.

All four of the branches of the military were each required to take an allotment of Critical Skills recruits. Of course the slots in the easy services (Air Force and Navy) filled up first. When it was my turn to choose, only the Army and the Marines had openings. Since it was the Army that I was trying to avoid, (besides, anyone could get into the Army) I picked the Marines. I was allowed to chose where I was going but had no control over when I would start my training.

A week before graduation[34] from IIT, my number came up and I was summoned to go to Parris Island, SC and start my 90-day military career. It was the first time I had ever been on an airplane. It was a short flight — from Chicago's Midway Airport to Columbia, SC.

Several of us were met at the airport by a drill instructor who seemed demented in his zeal to scream irrational orders at us. The trip to the Training Center in Parris Island took several hours on a government-furnished bus. We rode along two-lane country roads all the way to the coast because there were no interstate highways back then.

My recollection of the bus trip is limited to listening to the moronic DI and simultaneously being stunned by the magnitude of the squalid poverty I could see through the bus's windows. I do not know which impressed me more. It was my first trip to the Deep South and I didn't know people could live under such horrible conditions. The part that disturbed me the most was the shacks and the people were all in plain sight right there along the road, so the conditions I saw must not have been that unusual.

It turned out that the Marines did not get many Critical Skill enrollees, so the dozen or so of us were thrown in with the rest of the rabble. Our platoon consisted of a mix of about 70 guys, all different. Some very young and some old guys like me. There even were some who had never been outside of the county of their birth. Most of these guys were very poor and, I'm willing to bet, very few ever had any jobs or even Social Security numbers.

---

34 My last final exam was a take-home which I mailed just before I left for training. Fortunately, the Drill Instructors kept us very busy so I didn't have time to worry if I got a passing grade and actually did graduate — which I did.

We got the usual haircuts and the standard allotment of clothes, shoes, helmet, and other paraphernalia. It was an amazing and touching thing to see. One of the recruits from the hills of Tennessee cried when he was given a pair of shoes and a pair of combat boots. In his entire life he had never seen such a bounty much less possessed it. By the way, this same fellow — who had been shooting squirrels since he was six — did poorly on the rifle range because he just could not understand how to use an adjustable rifle sight. He relied on good ole' Kentucky Windage, which was okay when the squirrel was within 50 feet, but just didn't work well when the target was 500 yards away.

We were soon lined up on the parade ground, short to tall in three equal rows in the same platoon formation we would maintain throughout the training period. I found myself exactly in the middle of the front row; Right in front of the DI whenever we were being addressed. It simultaneously was the best place and the worst place. I certainly could hear and see everything but I also could readily be seen (and heard). I also became the most accessible target for visiting officers who came to perform inspections.

Soon after we got settled into our barracks, the DIs decided that it would be okay to humiliate the college boys, and permanent work assignments were made accordingly. Since I was a very recent college graduate, I was placed in charge of the toilet-cleaning crew. This actually turned out to be a good deal.

While everyone else was cleaning the barracks and being badgered full-time, my crew was left alone in our "special place." Also, since the standards for cleanliness were much lower for our detail, we only had to apply the minimum amount of effort, and that seemed to be good enough. We did scrub the toilets and floors daily, but that was easy and far better than what the others were doing; Moving all of the bunks and washing the wooded barracks floors several times over, sometimes with toothbrushes.

My biggest labor-saving breakthrough came when I discovered that the latrine's concrete floor had been scrubbed so many times in the past that there was a substantial amount of soap already embedded in the porous floor. We did not need to add any more soap, we could just scrub the floor directly with plain water and the excess soap from past generations would come up to the surface. Also, by using this method, the floor tended to dry quicker and looked shinier. We worked less and the DI was always satisfied. As a byproduct I was being inadvertently schooled in the ways of the military. What a nice arrangement.

The DIs' campaign to belittle the critical skills guys also didn't work as they had expected. Most of the other recruits were from farming communities, less than 18-years-old and away from home for the first time. They not only looked up to us because we were older, but also because we were mostly big-city guys who obviously knew more about life. So, instead of turning against us as the DIs had hoped, they turned toward us for help. I remember writing their letters home and reading the responses. In addition, we also served as their off-hour tutors for some of the military courses we were being taught.

Among the first things the military does in everyone's military career is to establish each recruit's level of physical ability. I was prepared for this phase. While others strained to demonstrate a high-level of performance, I "managed" to do very few push-ups, sit-ups, etc. Then, as time went on and our performance was again measured, I demonstrated a remarkable improvement each time. Cousin Walter's Post Office advice proved to be correct: when starting on any government job, always go slowly at first.

In addition to the physical testing we were also given an IQ test. The questions consisted of the usual; Word-recognition, spatial-understanding, a little math and some logic problems. I came away with almost a perfect score. I missed only one answer, mainly because I didn't get back to that question in-time.

Not surprisingly, all of the Critical Skills guys scored high on the test as well. Soon after the results were in, those with perfect and near-perfect scores were called out and marched over to visit with a Recruitment Officer. His task was to talk us into enlisting for a full six-year service. In exchange for this commitment we would be eligible to go to Quantico, VA and train as Marine pilots. This sounded wonderful.

I was very tempted to sign up. In retrospect I now can see this truly was a fork in the path of my life. Had I taken that road and became a Marine pilot, everything about my life would have changed — and not necessarily for the better or even for the worst. I still fantasize about that choice that wasn't made and a life that wasn't lived. I can only imagine my other self being a star in Top Gun school. After that it would only be natural for me to become a test pilot and finally an Astronaut. It would/could all have been so cool. But, I didn't do it, and it didn't happen.

Why didn't I sign up? Because when I asked the officer "what happens if I wash out of Flight School?" He told me I would then revert to the rank of Sergeant and remain in the service for the remainder of the six-year commitment.

Wrong answer!

If he had said that I would then be discharged (promoted to civilian, actually), I know I would have signed up. But, I wanted a guarantee, and they just don't issue them in the military.

Even though it was against regulations, I kept a small diary of my adventures at Parris Island. Almost every day I would make an entry or a paragraph or two into a small notebook which I kept hidden among my gear. On the cover I wrote the title in large bold letters, *Double Time to Nowhere*.

Predictably, it was soon discovered during a routine inspection and was forwarded to the officer in charge. Fortunately for me, I did not name names very often, and when I did, it was in a semi-complimentary manner. The Captain liked what he read, and when he personally returned it to me, he asked to see it again when it was finished. I lied when I agreed to hand it over at the end of boot camp.

Once in a class on M1 rifle theory and maintenance, I was incredibly bored because the instructor repeated the same material just too many times. The instructor could see from his vantage point I was not paying attention because my head was down for an extended period of time. He probably thought I was writing a letter and not listening.

He was half-right because, to keep from dozing off, I decided to draw an exploded-view drawing of the weapon. (This type of drawing was part of the job I had prior to boot camp.) He stormed over to my seat and snatched the paper out from under my pencil. I must say, he was quite surprised to see I had prepared a very detailed rendition of the very subject he was teaching.

When we were finally issued our rifles, I could see from my weapon's serial number (it had one digit less than the others) it was much older than anyone else's. Consequently, it had to be cleaned almost continuously to keep the rust from taking over. Because it was so old, the spring on the butt plate door — behind which the cleaning kit was stored — was very weak and the little door could be opened very easily. Once, when a Colonel came by for inspection, he picked me as a representative candidate. He took my rifle and gave it the usual look-and-spin. The speed of the spin was too much for the door spring and the Colonel launched the entire contents of the cleaning kit up into the air and down upon the heads of the platoon.

The rods and pieces made a great sound as they fell on the helmets of the giggling troops. Of course I couldn't laugh even though it was very funny. I stood frozen looking straight ahead, just a few inches away from the Colonel. As he closed the now empty butt chamber door and returned the rifle, he commented, "old rifle." "Yes sir," I replied. What a good Marine.

I thought for sure that the inspection episode would cause me to be issued a newer rifle. No such luck. The DIs loved the show and began to steer all future inspectors my way just to see a repeat performance.

Our head DI must have taken a liking to me because he designated me as Company Runner. This meant that I would sit in the

Captain's office when he was absent and I would answer the phone and respond to inquiries.

This was a good job! I not only did not have to participate in the make-work activities of the rest of the platoon, but I could secretly go through the desk drawers and learn what we would be doing next in our training sequence. Not only did I learn a lot in advance, but I could place guaranteed winning bets with other recruits. Not quite up to the Sgt. Bilko level, but not bad for a lowly Private.

My biggest money-winning bet was not made as a result of snooping but because I knew a little about statistics. I made a simple bet with a recruit that there would be two recruits in the platoon who had the exact same birthday. With a population of 70 random individuals, this is almost an absolute certainty. (Only about 25 people are required for the odds to be better than 50/50.)

Well, not only did the kid take the bet, but others wanted a piece of the action. After I got about $30 worth of betting interest, I conducted a survey among the platoon members and located not just one but several sets of coincidental birthdays plus one case of three on the same day! Easy money.

Sunday morning was a prime time for conducting harmless, make-work exercises for the recruits. This was necessary because the various denominations all used the same building for religious services and everyone could not go to church at the same time. This was a wonderful opportunity for spending a restful morning.

To avoid all of these foolish mess-kit cleaning, bayonet sharpening, shoe shinning drills I tried to attend multiple church services, one after the other. When discovered and questioned, I replied that I was seeking the true religion. The DI did not buy that and made me choose just one.

Even though all of the DIs smoked cigarettes, they did not want the troops to smoke. They discouraged it as much as possible by being openly intolerant of smokers. Nevertheless, several times a day they would make a concession and announce that the "smoking lamp was lit." All of the smokers would then fall out, stand in a circle near a dumpster and light up.

I did not smoke at the time but took it up just because it irritated the DIs. In fact, I tried to get everyone in the entire platoon to fall out and stand there holding a lighted butt. However, they were too chicken and wouldn't play. After a while, dealing with the other smokers became a bore and I easily kicked my phony habit.

For some unknown reason our platoon's training sequence ended five days short of the agree-upon 90 days. All of the real Marine recruits were transferred out to their next assignments while the Critical Skills guys were left behind to complete our military obligations.

Since we had finished basic training we could not be put into another platoon. Instead we were sent to Casual Company, which is where active personnel go temporarily between assignments.

Casual Company was located some distance from the Recruit training sites. Even though we were still on the base, it was a wonderful assignment. We had not responsibilities whatsoever nor were we assigned to an officers or non-coms.

We were free to sleep longer, wander around the rest of the base (including our old training sites), plus we had full-time access to both the swimming pool and the commissary bar. Uncle Sam not only subsidized our nightly beer purchases but also provided the necessary aspirins the next morning.

Just before we were released from active duty, an officer who was in charge of Public Relations interviewed some of the departing CSers. One of the guys was asked "what did you get out of your tour of duty here at Parris Island?" To which he replied: "The best suntan I ever had." He then quickly added "Sir." How soon we forget.

Something humorous/serious/weird happened almost every day, but none of these other incidents are worthy of mention, except one.

Of the 70 or so recruits who comprise a platoon, two or three of the outstanding ones are usually moved up in rank to Private First Class at the end of boot camp. I can't claim to have been an outstanding recruit, but I somehow must have fooled a lot of people because, when I went back home to Chicago, I not only had been promoted to civilian, but I also had a PFC stripe on my sleeve.

PERSPECTIVE: Sure I was in the Marines. Sure I have a DD-214 (discharge paper) to prove it. But there's this gut feeling I get when I answer "yes" to the question: "were you ever in the military?" I always feel I need to clarify what happened. If I don't explain, I feel like a fraud.

18

Adventures

When I was in about third grade I was given a small globe of the earth. I was very fascinated to see how far Poland was from Chicago and to see how really big the earth was. I also learned that Chicago occupied only a very small fraction of the earth's surface, and was not the center of anything, much less the universe. It was then that I realized there were many other places one could visit and live. Chicago was only my accidental starting point. I wanted to go see the other places.

Over the next few years I compiled a mental list of the places I wished to go some day. The list got longer as I came in contact with magazines such as the *National Geographic.* By the time I got to high school, my list was almost complete. It contained the following locations: Yellowstone National Park, San Francisco, Disneyland, Rio de Janeiro, Italy, Greece, and Egypt.

Several interesting things about this list are the many places it didn't contain. Why not Poland? Or New York? Or Switzerland? No idea, but that was my list and, as an adult, I've managed to visit all of them — all except Egypt. I'm saving that trip for my last journey. When I finally do travel there, it'll probably be all over for me.

"See the pyramids and die" should be my motto.

In addition to visiting the far-away places mentioned above, I did have a few local adventures, one of which involved F&F,[35] and also Ralph. Just for the heck of it, the four of us decided to go on a camping trip to Northern Minnesota.

This was, indeed, more of an accomplishment than it appears on the surface. None of us had been Boy Scouts and no one had ever slept in a tent, much less paddled a canoe. There were so many things we didn't know about the outdoors it's pointless to try and list them. We were real city rubes out in the bush. But somehow we survived ten days alone in the lakes and woods without severe injuries.

We arranged the trip through an outfitter who supplied all of the equipment and the food. We only brought clothes, fishing gear and booze. Well, it turns out we didn't bring enough of any category listed. First we ran out of booze — probably on the first day. Then all of the clothes got wet when a canoe tipped. And finally, a medium-sized bear came along and ate most of the food.

So, there we were, very far from the launch point and nothing to eat except a few canned goods. We commenced serious fishing because that was the only option left.

This is where my chicken-processing skills came in handy. Although the insides of a chicken are very different from that of a

---

35 I mentioned Frank-n-Flo in a previous chapter.

fish, all anatomy is based on the same principles. We all caught the fish and I would fillet them and do the cooking. It all worked out well.

Ralph and I were involved in another weird adventure when we went to New Orleans for the 1958 Mardi Gras. We had no reservations. We just took off on a Sunday morning and headed south from Chicago. There were four of us in Ralph's ten-year-old Cadillac.

This was during the pre-interstate highway days, so the trip was made over two-lane roads. We all took turns driving, including me, the only one without a driver's license. It was my turn to drive after dark on the first night out. The others fell asleep almost as soon as I got behind the wheel without knowing the danger they were in.

There was very little or no traffic on that narrow country road somewhere in southern Indiana (or maybe even Kentucky), so it was easy for an amateur driver to stay to the right of the white line. Soon a light snow began to fall. It quickly covered the highway and, since there was no traffic in front of me, I had nothing to guide me: no white line, tail-lights, or even tire tracks. However, I could faintly see the barbed wire fence posts on both sides of the road and so I simply stayed half-way between them and pressed on further south.

I drove like this for several hours until we finally passed from under the weak storm. When I proudly relayed my navigational accomplishment at dawn, I was yelled at and not allowed to drive unsupervised at night again. Too bad, I thought I had done very well.

The subject changed quickly when the new driver noticed that we were almost out of gas. (Another small detail that escapes amateurs.) We were quite far from a major city and, although all of the little towns we passed through had gas stations, none were open at that hour.

Half of us wanted to press on until the car ran out of fuel, and the other half wanted to park in a closed gas station and wait for it to open. Ralph was in the later group and since it was his car, his side won.

We pulled into the next gas station and parked near the pumps. I got out and discovered there was still some gas left in the hose after the pump was turned off. Not much gas; maybe a pint, but certainly more than we had in the tank.

So that's when we put Plan B into operation.

We drove on, stopped at every closed station we encountered and emptied all of the free "hose gas" into our tank. A few miles down the road we found a station that was open and solved the problem.

The downside of this procedure was that the very first person to draw gas after the station opened got short-changed by a hose-full of gas. But, at the then price 29 cents a gallon, it wasn't much of a theft.

When we finally got to New Orleans, Ralph found a parking spot on Jackson Square, right in the center of the French Quarter. Incredible! The car stayed parked for the next several days and we all took turns sleeping in it. (No point in even trying to find a hotel room.)

It was then that I stayed up all night for the first time in my life and just wandered alone throughout the Quarter, taking in the sights and sounds. I had never before seen the likes of this revelry and nothing can ever impress me in the same way again because it could not be seen through those same innocent eyes.

I took movies of our stay but they were all terrible. I had only recently bought the camera and did not really know how to use it. I moved the camera far too much and too fast. The last time I watched the films I got a major headache.

While in NO we drank a lot of beer and the beer-of-choice was named JAX. It was produced by a local brewery situation on the river front so I can only image where the water came from. Anyway, this beer tasted wonderful. Each can was better than the last. It was so good we all decided to take some home with us.

After a few days back in Chicago, I decided to relive some of my experiences and opened a can. It was horrible! Poured it all out. Not surprisingly, 99 percent of the "great-beer taste" came from our own imaginations.

My last big adventure happened when F&F and I rented a 29-foot cabin cruiser for a week and drove it around the southern end of Lake Michigan. It was a well-equipped boat with many sleeping compartments, a head, galley and two large engines.

I still cannot believe the rental agency would lease a brand new boat to some totally inexperienced people like us. I still did not have a driver's license but I was allowed to drive a huge boat!

The only lesson we got in navigation and operation was during the 30-minute run on the Chicago River out to the Lake. We then proceeded to learn what to do by trial and error. Mostly error it turns out.

To dock the boat, we simply crashed it into the pier, cut the engine, and someone jumped off with a rope and pulled the boat in. We scratched the hell out of that craft, plus I ran also over the anchor chain and damaged a propeller.

Another thing was that we couldn't handle the slow pace of a boat. We didn't realize that they barely move through the water. We had such ambitions of going everywhere. All we ended up doing was going across the lake to Benton Harbor, Michigan, turning around and coming back.

Oh, we did stop at a few other harbors along the way and dorked around at the waterfront bars, but the entire journey was basically a costly disappointment, especially when the bill for the damages was presented.

PERSPECTIVE: If you were expecting a longer or even a racier list, I'm sorry, but that's all I've got. By now you should know that, at this point in life, I didn't have; the means, the money, or even the know-how to have grander escapades. Believe me, I'm disappointed too.

19

Obituary

Well, it finally happened — after several false endings, John A. Marszalek has completed his long earthen journey. Now mind you, it's not that he wanted to go. He was perfectly happy to go on living.

And why shouldn't he?

He was a very lucky man. He lived his whole adult life in the company of beautiful, intelegent women (his wife and daughters), had enough money to do whatever he wanted to do, and he had a well-oiled sense-of-humor. His life was a long and pleasant journey.

He came from a humble background wherein work was an integral part of life. Consequently he felt he had to be somehow employed all of the time. At an early age he worked as a delivery boy for a grocery store and also delivered newspapers. Then later, while attending IIT, he was a weekend lecturer at the Museum of Science and Industry in Chicago. Here he learned to stand before a large group of people — strangers, really — and deliver a message. This ability proved very valuable in all of his future assignments.

John did a lot of other interesting things in his life, mostly when he had "real" jobs. He was lucky enough to be a pioneer in the field of electronics and computer design back when no one else knew exactly what they were doing which allowed John to fit right in unnoticed.

He probably had far too many job entries on his resume. Thus situation was not because he couldn't keep a job for a long time, but because he got bored after the new technology became common place and decided it was time to move on to something newer.

It's just as well he did move around because most of the companies where he had worked have gone out-of-business. He liked to believe that he could see the end coming and would try to be the first to get out. His favorite expression in this regard was "the rats watch me to see if the ship is sinking."

In his 40-year career as an engineer he was only laid-off twice, and in both cases he had another job lined-up down the street. But things were much different then when even a C- engineer could easily get a job. (His other favorite expression was "I graduated in the top 100% of my class.")

While working on different classified projects he was granted several levels of security, some above Top Secret. He would have liked to tell you about some of these tasks but didn't want to get into trouble. (Not that it would matter at this point.)

John's most adventurous job took him and his family to Brazil for two years where he worked with local authorities helping to expand the operation of a computer-control installation that ran an existing subway system.

His final "real" job was working as a consultant with the FAA in Washington DC. This position enabled him to observe air traffic controllers in action and inspired the idea for a labor-saving aid for the controllers. He subsequently applied for and received a patent for the idea but could not sell the concept for several reasons; primarily because its implementation would interfere with the retirement plans of many FAA organization heads.

After his own retirement he was fortunate to put his museum-lecturing background to work by getting a teaching assignment at a community college teaching introductory electrical engineering classes.

John also had a stint in the military, but it was just a stint; in fact, a very short stint. Back when the draft was still in effect, he was classified as 1-A; the next to be called. However, because of his security level job at the time he was granted the deferred classification of "Critically Skilled."

This allowed him to avoid the draft by serving only 90 days in the Marines followed by an eight-year commitment in the Standby Reserves. (Basically a non-commitment since he did not have to attend reserve meetings or go on annual training missions.) He was both proud and embarrassed by his military history and felt badly that he never did find out how he would act in a real battle situation.

Some of his outstanding non-job achievements included designing and actually building portions of the family's home and constructing at least a dozen decks and patios in three different states.

He and his wife Janet traveled extensively after retirement. They preferred to visit faraway places as travelers not as tourists. This involved renting an apartment or a house in some foreign land and then living among the locals. However, as time went by they did relent and did go on tours, but this was never their preferred mode of travel.

But all that was in the past, and now he's gone.

Farewell.

Addendum

As stated previously, we played many games other than sports. None of these activities needed electronic assistance which is just as well, since such luxuries did not exist. Almost all of these games were group-efforts with as many as six or more participants. Thus, by playing together, we learned how to socialize, how to win and also, how to lose.

Street Games

Street games came in two varieties — those that needed a "drawing" and those that did not. Both are described below.

After it was agreed upon what game to play (which sometimes would involve a long period of negotiation and rules-clarification), a level location on the street was selected. If a game drawing was needed, a suitable stone had to be found in a nearby empty lot since we rarely had any chalk even though it was readily stealable from school. (For some reason it was something one just didn't do.)

The game's pattern, which usually consisted of a series of rectangles or boxes, would be drawn in the middle of the street and a game played by any number of participants. We often played Sky Blue (a.k.a. Hopscotch) and roly-poly, a game I have not ever seen played anywhere since leaving grade school.

Rules for Roly-Poly

This was the most popular of all the street games. It taught us hand-eye coordination and was an exercise in memory retention, both of which could later serve as useful traits in old age.

A large rectangle is drawn on a reasonably flat part of the street and then divided into two vertical columns of smaller rectangles or boxes, each about one foot by two feet. Any number of boxes can be used, but the practical limit is about eight (two columns of four). Each box is assigned a different category such as: cars, boy names, girl names, colors, etc as shown below.

Note the inclusion of cigarette names. For some reason when we were ten-year-olds we knew a minimum of eight brands of cigarettes. What does that tell you?)

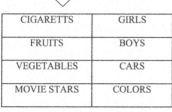

CIGARETTS	GIRLS
FRUITS	BOYS
VEGETABLES	CARS
MOVIE STARS	COLORS

REVERSE   START

The game is played by one player at a time with all other players watching and listening intently. Play begins at the designated "start" corner of the large rectangle, typically, the lower right.

A tennis ball is rolled by the player toward box number one and must be immediately picked up when the player steps into the box while standing on only one foot. This is easy for the first box because it requires the player to take only a single step, bend down and catch the rolling ball. Later in the game, the difficulty increases substantially.

Upon picking up the ball, the player announces the category written in the box — in this example, "Colors," a good category for box number one.

The player now advances, without stopping, through all of the other boxes placing only one foot in each, bouncing the tennis ball once per box and reciting a single item from the category; For example; red, white, blue, green, yellow, purple etc.

Because there were fewer colors back then, everyone had to use the same ones. We did not know about puce, chartreuse or magenta, but some clever kids did use white, tan and gray, which aren't really colors, but were somehow acceptable.

In preparation for the game, each player had memorized his own sequence within each category. If I had to do the colors category now, I'd use the sequence "red, orange, yellow, green, blue, indigo and violet," the primary spectral colors of the rainbow. I didn't know anything about this trick at the time.

After successfully traversing all the boxes, the player spins around on one foot in the last box, bounces the ball once, repeats the last named item and then does the entire sequence in reverse all the way around to the first box. While doing so, all of the item names just used must be repeated in their exact reverse sequence. How did we know when we made a mistake? All of the other player/observers would tell us, that's how.

If the reverse sequence has been executed correctly, the player goes to the start corner and rolls the ball towards box number two, moves forward to catch it and recites the items from category two. This goes on until a item-sequence mistake is made, a line is stepped on, or the rolled ball is not picked up in the targeted box.

(You've probably noticed that ball rolling and catching becomes quite difficult when working the second column of boxes. Also, the number of items recited/memorized per category is not the same for all boxes. "Colors" needs a full eight going forward and also eight going in reverse whereas "Boys" needs only six going forward and a full eight in reverse.

Many variations were also available in addition to the layout. One-handed ball catching was one. Bouncing the ball (ala basketball dribbling) without catching it was a fast-paced, brutal version. There were other more-advanced rules such as box ownership which I won't go into. (If you "owned" a box, other players could not step into it.)

Games that did not need drawings were, of course, easier to set up. The most popular of these was called "three feet in the mud." All this required was about twenty feet of clear curbing on opposite sides of the street. As I said before, the streets were empty of parked cars so this requirement was easy to fulfill.

Rules for Three Feet in the Mud

Two border markers were selected that outlined a playing field. These borders could be a fireplug on one side and a sewer cover on the other, or maybe a lamp post.

One person was "it" and stood in the middle of the street. All other players stood on a curb. The "it" kid would issue a command such as "take two steps," and everyone would leap from the curb.

Once off of the curb, the object was to run to the other side without being tagged by the "it" kid. A player could stand still or move laterally and still be safe, but could not make a break towards the other side without danger of being caught. When a player was tagged, he joined the "it" guy in the middle and tried to capture the other players.

It was a simple game requiring a little speed and possibly some cunning. The secret was to get the boundaries just right for the number of players or else it just didn't work well.

One variation was that those who made it across could "rescue" the others by racing back and touching them. Once contact was made, both were safe, but the potential savior was taggable during the reverse flight.

After taking the commanded number of steps off of the curb, the players could also inch forward a bit when unseen by the "it" kid. If the "it" kid suspected that a played had moved forward too much, he would call a halt to the game, mark the spot where the player stood and the player would be challenged to get to that spot in the same number of steps that had been commanded. Failure to do so is the same as being tagged.

Choosing Sides

Deciding who would be on each team for softball or other games was always an interesting socio-political exercise. Everyone wanted to be on the winning side, but the sides had to be more or less equal to be fair. The least popular method — if you were a poor player — was to have the two best players take turns selecting from the pool. This was very bad for the egos of the last few selected.

Another was the "one potato, two potato" method. Kids apparently believed that this little poem somehow produced a random selection of participants. It consisted of chanting this (meaningless) little mantra while pointing, in sequence, to each candidate player:

one potato, two potato, three potato, four,
five potato, six potato, seven potato, more

The word "more" designated the selected player. (Don't ask why. That's just the way it was.)

Of course there was nothing random about this method. The first person selected was simply eight places removed from the first one. I figured this out early and, depending upon how many players were present and who was chanting/pointing, I knew exactly where to stand to be picked first — or even last, for that matter.

Asphalt Art

We also used the street for other more sedentary activities that were not really games but ways to pass the time. In the heat of summer when the asphalt was quite soft and could be easily carved, we would sit right in the center of the street and gouge figures, names, and even personal insults into the surface using our ever-available pocket knives. However, due to the intense heat of summer, the tar would slowly flow and the images would disappear long before the start of the next new school year. In a very short time the street was left smooth again, ready to accept the work of next summer's artisans.

It's too bad that these works of art could not be preserved for viewing and analysis by future sociologists. They could have served as a modern version of the Lascaux cave paintings.

Dirt Games

Some games were played in the dirt between the curb and the sidewalk. These were generally less violent and typically designed for a smaller number of players. Mild games like "marbles" were periodically very popular, and then interest would wane for a few weeks only to reappear with newly discovered fervor.

Knife games also were also played on these curbside playing fields. Soft dirt was required, however, so these were not played during the hot, dry summer months.

The standard form of mumbly-peg was popular, as was "splits." The later required a good deal of knife-throwing skill. It also required considerable foresight and agility to compensate for the other player's lack of knife-throwing skills.

Rules for Splits

Two players stood facing each other an arm's length apart with both feet together. From a full standing position, player number one would try to stick his knife into the ground next to the other kid's foot. If it stuck and if it was within a predetermined distance — usually the length of a knife blade — the targeted foot would be moved next to the stuck knife.

After moving his foot, it would be kid number two's turn to throw his knife at (actually, near) a foot of player number one. This back-and-forth throw, stick, and move sequence continued until one of the guys "split" and fell down.

The agility part of the game involved knowing when to move a targeted foot out of the way to keep it from being jabbed. I guess we were either accurate knife-throwers or fast-foot-movers because hardly anyone got stuck.

Other games were played outdoors but were typically enjoyed under-cover on a shaded front porch. Here we spent our rainy or extremely hot afternoons playing cards or board games. The most popular card game was "knuckles" — as described in Chapter 9 — followed by "crazy-8" and, when we were really bored, "war."

Another popular activity was pitching pennies. Even though the name of the game pretty much says it all, here's a description of it anyway.

Rules for Pitching Pennies

A line (the expansion groove in the concrete) on a sidewalk is designated as the target line. Two or more participants stand two or more concrete squares away from the line and take turns pitching one penny at a time to see whose coin lands closest to the target line.

After all players have tossed a pre determined number of coins (this could be one-at-a-time or even as many as five), the players move forward and examine the resulting coin pattern. A judgment is made as to which penny is the closest to the line and that player picks up all of the coins. If any of the coins happens to come to rest in the line (grove), or straddles the line, that player collects double the amount from each player.

One variation on the game was that if a coin landed above the line, it would be disqualified and not count in the scoring. This version required considerable skills and was seldom played.

There is quite an art in knowing how to pitch a coin. Some tossed them so that they would land flat and maybe bounce very little. Others flipped theirs with the hope that the spinning action would somehow lessen the bounce. The really artful — and seldom realized — toss was to make the penny land on its edge, bounce just a little, and then roll forward to end up in the line/grove.

You can only imagine how dinged-up these pennies became after being bounced off of the concrete for a few hours. Some of them got to be so badly damaged that even the corner candy store guy would not accept them as payment.

I also remember watching some of the bigger guys play the game, but with higher stakes: they would usually pitch nickels or even quarters. This was much too rich for my crowd. (By the way, dimes were seldom if ever tossed. They are far too small and light and just don't bounce right.)

Outdoor games that required more room than the street could afford were played in the prairie. As stated before, this is strictly a Chicago term that has probably long since gone out of use. It referred to an empty lot. A city lot was typically 25-feet wide and about 100-feet-deep — hardly the place to be called a prairie, but that's what we called it.

Because they were untended (except for some kids' feet stomping here and there), these lots had lots of weeds growing in them by mid-summer. These weeds were not the semi-friendly, ground-hugging variety found in suburban lawns. The prairies had huge green weeds that had trunks instead of stalks. You could practically carve your initials in them. They resembled bamboo in thickness, density and height. They formed our private little playgrounds wherein we recreated Tarzan movie adventures and Pacific island war battles.

Even though prairies were empty, they did belong to someone who paid the taxes. No matter. We looked upon them as if they were our own. We built forts in them, had rock fights, and played softball in the larger ones. In other words, that's where all of the good things happened.

The problem was that we also were very dependent upon them, and we were highly insulted (and disappointed) when the owner of our favorite prairie began building a house on it. The nerve! Our ball field was ruined by a huge foundation in right field. The really bad part was, after a month of work on the site, the project was abandoned. We tried, at first, to get rid of this eyesore by attempting to break the concrete projecting out of the ground but to no avail. We had lost our field forever.

Board Games

Of course we played a few board games, but not very often. The most popular games were Checkers and Parcheesi. As kids we lacked the attention spans required to play and finish complex games like Monopoly, so these games were seldom played even though they may have been available.

Index

Chapter 4:

My mother dressed in one of her homemade Polish costumes.

Chapter 6:

That's me with some kid from the neighborhood.

Chapter 12:

Front steps of Saint Francis of Assisi church and school.

Chapter 14:

I'll in my basement "lab" trying to get something electrical to work.

High school graduation photo.

Chapter 17:

A Marine Corps recruitment photo if I ever saw one.